thinking. Ricci's book provides an easy, quantitative tool to measure day-to-day growth exposure. By focusing on the journey instead of end-game achievements, *The Growth Game* helps the reader to identify early in the process the opportunities that will fuel and stall growth, allowing the reader to create his or her own road map to success."

-   Jenn Dlugos, Award winning author, screenwriter and writing professor

"In this informational gem, Ricci shows you how to become brilliant at the basics so you can shine professionally and thrive by increasing your capacity to perform at optimal levels."

-   Machen MacDonald, Founder of FroBrilliance Leadership Institute

DAD⊕
point tracker

To subscribe to the DAD System software that is
discussed throughout this book and for any updated
content please visit our website.

www.thegrowthgame.com

"Eddy Ricci is a forward thinker who speaks from his mind and his heart and the results always exceed one's expectations—his voice is of a true original."

- Andrew Goldman, HBO- Vice President of Program Planning

"Eddy Ricci understands what motivates Gen Y sales teams. He's on my radar and should be on yours!"

- Erik Qualman, #1 Best Selling author and International Keynote Speaker [Founder of Socialnomics and # 2 most likable author behind J.K Rowling]

"Ricci is the emerging expert in developing Generation Y professionals. He possesses a rare blend of high creativity, strong business skills and an ability to connect with people."

- Linda Kaplan Thaler, Chairman of Publicis Kaplan Thaler [Advertising executive responsible for *The Aflack Duck*, *Kodak Moments* and the *Toys R Us jingle* campaigns and guest mentor of various reality shows such as *The Apprentice*.]

"After you frame your diploma, you must read *The Growth Game*. Ricci has delivered a dynamic system that focuses on YOUR passion for the process to drive results I wish I was given the book after graduation. Be prepared for YOUR greatness."

- Ben Newman, International speaker and author of the National Bestseller *Own YOUR Success*

"*The Growth Game* makes professional development fun, exciting and rewarding. Ricci pushes you to earn your way to a successful career, while supporting you along the way with advice and expert tips."

- Dan Schawbel, Bestselling author of Me 2.0 and Promote Yourself [Founder of Millennial Partners and contributing writer for Forbes.com]

"*The Growth Game* is a great tool for young professionals to think about their life goals: personal and professional-beyond their educational career. Once school advisors are no longer available, professionals can look to the book to help shape their path and validate their everyday activities as a step toward their future."

- Stephanie Dara Posen, New York University-Senior Development

"Eddy Ricci has developed a brilliant 'token economy' system to enable young professionals to track progress towards their personal and professional goals on a daily basis. This system is applicable to anyone looking to hold themselves accountable to their own professional growth and development."

- Joey Davenport, International Speaker and Principal of Hoopis Performance Network

"Up until now, we have measured personal and professional growth by achievements. Most of the time, we do not even know we have grown until we hit a certain milestone. Eddy Ricci's *The Growth Game* changes this

The Growth Game

A Millennial's Guide to Professional Development and The DAD System

✚

Eddy Ricci, Jr.

No part of this book may be copied or reproduced without
permission. For permissions and information:
info@thegrowthgame.com
The Growth Game, LLC.

www.thegrowthgame.com

Library of Congress Cataloguing To Be Filed

WGA-East 2012

Copyright © 2013

Cover design by Sean P. Donnelly

ISBN: 0615801978
ISBN-13: 978-0615801971

For My Parents
In Loving Memory of My Father

Contents

Acknowledgements   vii

Foreword by Alan Weiss, PhD   ix

Introduction   xi

Section One: The Growth Game   1

Chapter One: The DAD System 3

Chapter Two: Score Keeping 11

Chapter Three: The Future Workforce 25

Section Two: Internal Development   39

Chapter Four: Affirmations to Activities 41

Chapter Five: Silencing Your EGA   51

Chapter Six: Information Epidemic   59

<u>Section Three: People</u> 67

Chapter Seven: Expanding Connections 69

Chapter Eight: Professionalism and the
Third- First Impression 81

Chapter Nine: Human Connectivity 95

Concluding Summary 113

Games to Play 117

FAQ 123

Notes 127

About the Author 129

-Acknowledgements-

I wanted to first thank my wonderful family for all that they do. I am truly blessed to be around such caring people. Thank you to my mother for all her years of selflessness and sacrifice. To my beautiful wife, Laurie, who sees all sides of me and still puts up with me. And for a supportive group of siblings who I love, Dana, Nina, Nikki, Glen, Eric and Jim and their children Nathan, Zachary, EJ, Matthew, Diana and Francesca.

I am very fortunate to work with four leaders who I have learned so much from, both directly and by observation. They do not get thanked enough so I want to express my gratitude to Dave McAvoy, Bob Frieling, Scott Christensen and Jeff Zuzolo.

Thank you to those leaders that have had an influence on me over my career, especially Cristi Stroud. Thank you to Adam Seiden, Joey Davenport and Mike Matone. There are many other people who have helped me in my career but it would be impossible to list them all.

To some friends and partners who always provide support and perspective: Michael Connaughton, Nate Catucci, Alesh Hlozek, and Guy Asacorian. Thank you, Sean Donnelly for the cover design.

Thank you to Jenn Dlugos and Gabbie Cirelli for editing a messy manuscript and to Ryan Graff for his software expertise. Finally, thank you to Erik Qualman and Alan Weiss for having a contagious passion for what they do.

- Foreword-

To Grow Or Not To Grow?
That's really not a question!

I've counseled and coached thousands of executives and entrepreneurs all over the globe. Despite culture, climate, and configuration, one constant emerges: You grow or you die.

There is no such psychological topography as a "healthy plateau." Because of the laws of entropy, all plateaus eventually erode, along with everything comfortably resting on them. To live is to grow, and to thrive is to grow assertively.

The best people I've encountered are always looking for new ways, new directions, new experiences, new learning. They are educationally peripatetic, in that their inertia is to be an object in motion, not an object at rest.

However, we all need help to assertively grow. We need "fresh air" to prevent breathing our own exhaust, no matter how good we are. Outside stimuli and opinions are important to spur growth, to calibrate the climb, and to understand when we need to rest and when we need to continue the journey.

In this insightful book, Eddy Ricci, Jr. uses his pragmatic business experience coupled with a resourceful, simple system to provide that external prompting. He's the guide on the journey, and he's packing a compass, carabiners, ropes, pulleys, and oxygen to enable you to climb farther and faster.

Our choice is to grow or stagnate. That's not much of a choice. But this journey isn't about reaching the mountaintop. If you follow Eddy's advice, the sky is the limit.

— Alan Weiss, PhD
— Author, *Million Dollar Consulting, The Consulting Bible* and 46 other books.

-Introduction-

Am I growing?

It doesn't matter if this question is addressed professionally or personally, we all want to answer with a yes. If you asked yourself this question right now, how would you answer? If you answered "yes," then how are you tracking and analyzing your growth on a daily basis? If you answered "no," what activities are you conducting daily to put yourself into a position to grow? Or perhaps you are in the majority of people who answered this question with "I don't know."

As humans, we crave growth, but many of us don't perceive it until after it has occurred. We tend to see growth as an end result. A job title, salary raise, award, or degree are all evidence that we have grown, but we fail to notice and dissect the exposure to growth that accelerated us to the achievement. In most cases, our growth was a product of the things that we learned and the people that we met. How impactful would it be if we had a system that allowed us to score how productive each day was toward our longer term personal or professional development?

Much of the content in this book is adapted from my experience in the financial services industry. I was fortunate enough to start my career with a college internship at an industry leading company. I chose this internship because I knew the skills I would learn would transfer to any career path I pursued. As I grew with the company, I became involved with its best-in-class training and leadership programs. Many companies have good programs, but certain dynamics of financial services make this one unlike those of other industries. While other businesses hang their success on better Internet searches, mastering tax codes or understanding the ins and outs of derivatives, our industry measures success based on relationships. Since the service we provide is intangible, mastering relationships and human understanding are crucial keys to success.

In working with over one thousand financial professionals in my young career— the majority of whom were building a business from scratch— I realized how valuable our professional development and sales training systems were. I also realized how applicable these concepts and methods are to any other field that relies on interacting with people and lifelong learning. Many times professionals and business owners are so brilliant and focused on their talents, product, or niche that implementing and updating development systems is often left on the back burner, or they simply do not know where to begin.

The concepts provided in this book, although most beneficial for young professionals, can help anyone seeking professional or personal growth in his or her life or business. For young professionals, *The Growth Game* can help you build real world skills that may have been absent in the traditional, academic world. The book can serve as a roadmap to upstart a business or career search that depends on meeting people. If you are an aspiring or current leader, this book can help you become aware of your own growth process and help you encourage growth in organization. Even students can benefit from the concepts by tracking who they are meeting and what they are learning with their career advisors, mentors, or parents to assist them in preparing for their future career.

Imagine a world where everyone can use the same measuring stick to score their self improvement, each day. The purpose of this book is to introduce you to the Daily Activities of Development (DAD) System that values the things you learn and the people you meet. The DAD System will help you to quantify your exposure to growth and encourages you to capture each day's activities for future reflection. The book will also review both time tested and time relevant tactics to enhance your learning and people - meeting skills to help you develop into the person, professional or leader that you want to become. Good luck in reading, playing and living *The Growth Game.*

Section One

The Growth Game

"You will be the same person in five years as you are today except for the people you meet and the books you read." - Charlie "Tremendous" Jones, Speaker and Author

A game, at its core, exists to provide its players or spectators some type of amusement. Games force us to make decisions— whether those decisions are based on luck or applying skill, they are often connected to a series of feelings based on the outcomes. Those feelings often provide opportunities for us to change. No matter if your game of choice is a physical sport, a board game, or a computer game. Games can help us learn, bring people together, relax us and keep our minds sharp. Almost anything in our world can either be looked at as part of a game or be turned into a game.

Growth is the increase of quantity over time. It's

usually easy to measure growth. Height is a simple measurement of physical growth in children. Investment growth can be measured by returns and the value of the asset. The growth of a city is measured by population or economic metrics. A website measures growth by the number of hits, followers, or advertising dollars. Businesses base growth on revenues or profits.

Humans dedicate their time, energy, and often their lives to making things grow. But how can we measure if we are actually growing or not on a day to day or week to week basis? Can you name three things that you did this past week that made you grow? In something as ambiguous as personal or professional growth, we typically label growth as an end result instead of having an awareness, appreciation, and strategy around the daily ingredients that lead us to the results. We label growth more as an output device versus appreciating and analyzing the input. If we become more conscious of these accumulating development ingredients, we can adjust and control the trajectory of our growth.

Section One will introduce the Daily Activities of Development (DAD) System for personal and professional development. You will learn about a growth exposure score-keeping system and how playing this game can help you throughout different stages of your career. Section One will also explain the different ways in which you can use the system and how it is relevant to the world's changing workforce.

-Chapter One-

The DAD System

I have spent much of my career with Northwestern Mutual, a 155-year-old financial services company. In almost every role I have had, my central focus was to work with professionals, from all different backgrounds, to help them start a financial services practice from scratch. This involved implementing time tested systems and creating innovative processes that are relevant today to help the advisors develop skill sets that are necessary in building a clientele.

One of the company's legends was a man named Al Granum. Granum was a Managing Partner in Chicago who conducted a revolutionary 25-year, data-gathering study on his financial professionals. The results of the study allowed him to create a blueprint for financial professionals that made the client acquisition cycle more predictable.

Granum's study showed that the average financial advisor has a 10-3-1 ratio of client acquisition. For every 10 referrals a professional receives, he or she will have in-depth, face-to-face meetings with three of these prospective clients. From those three meetings, one will result in a new client for the advisor. However, the one new client in the ratio may come over a three-year lag period.

Granum's study created a science to the profession. By the ratio alone, you can see the rejection and long-term mindset that is required to do well in the business. The financial services business has a large amount of delayed gratification. Therefore, it is impossible for a financial professional to judge how well he or she performed on a given day, just by the number of sales. Granum knew his professionals needed a measuring stick at the end of each day to determine if they completed enough business activity to sustain themselves in the future. To quantify it, he made a list of important activities and awarded point values to each one. Points were tallied at the end of each business day.

Some examples of Granum's "point generating" activities included obtaining a referral, gaining insight into a client's financial situation, and making a solutions-based presentation. Granum knew if a professional accrued enough activity points today, then the sales would come tomorrow. His point system quantitatively measured his financial professionals' daily exposure to the marketplace.

After the study, professionals met daily, weekly and monthly to analyze their activity points and dissect areas of opportunity. Instead of claiming a good or bad month, Granum's professionals had a recognizable, quantitative, and measurable point value of their market exposure. Even today, thirty years after the study, if you ask any Northwestern Mutual representative in the country how many points he or she had this month, he or she would know exactly what you are talking about.

Introducing the Daily Activities of Development (DAD) System

"How was your day?"

How do you respond to that question when asked by your spouse, parents, or children at the end of each day? How will the day you just completed affect your long term future? What if there was a point system in your daily life to allow you to answer these questions more clearly?

I developed the Daily Activities of Development (DAD) System when I became the director of training and development for a region of financial services firms. While the leaders in the company quantified the productivity of each advisor's day with the Granum system, I wanted to track my professional and personal growth with a system that was quantitative and flexible. I wanted a fun and reflective accountability mirror for my growth. Essentially, I wanted to challenge myself to a game.

Like the Granum system, the DAD System is a quantitative measuring and reflection tool. It tackles the delayed gratification aspect of personal or professional growth with a "points for activity" system that brings your awareness to the people and learning you need to accelerate your path. Unlike the Granum system, the DAD system is more theoretical and can be used by anyone from any industry who wants to be a better professional, build better habits, or just become aware of their growth patterns.

It was intentional that I chose an acronym that spelled DAD. Throughout my life, my father would always challenge me to grow. In high school, he would get upset if I was playing on a computer or by myself on a weekend, instead of being out with my friends or meeting people. He was big on constant learning. He would give me pop quizzes at 15-years-old to the tune of, "Name me three Supreme Court justices." Ouch.   Later on in my schooling, probably due to his influence, I became very extroverted. I was constantly networking and meeting new people. I also developed his passion for learning. Today, I find it both important and entertaining to read and watch media relevant to my career.

Motivational speaker Charlie "Tremendous" Jones once said, "You will be the same person in five years as you are today except for the people you meet and the books you read." Thanks to my father's influence, I subscribed to this theory and built the DAD System on those two crucial growth ingredients: people and learning.

The DAD System's scorekeeping system will keep you focused on the attention you give to growing your contacts and expanding your knowledge. It will provide you with positive reinforcement of your growth exposure. While we will be going into the system in depth in Chapter Two, below is an outline of activities that will earn you points.

Point Values

Activity	Point Value
Affirmations	1 points
Knowledge	Z (customized)
Growth Related Action (GRA) or New Experience	3 points
New Connections	.5 point
Relationship Builders	Z (customized)
Meals/Quality Time	1 point (additional)

The point values assigned to the chosen categories were based on a study where the participants needed to distribute 10 points depending how they felt after finishing the criteria of the six selected categories. The more growth they felt could come from the activity in the future, the higher the point value assigned. Without question, a sense of growth occurred most after they had a new experience or took action towards a certain goal, no matter if the experience was positive or negative. The least amount of growth was felt by attaining a new connection (whether introduced in person or by social media). The thinking was that there is a chance that you may never end up connecting or meeting with that person. After reading some comments, making observations, and reflecting on my experiences in working with financial professionals with the Granum system, I modified some categories and didn't use all 10 allowed points in the original study's disbursement.

"A" Guide For Using The DAD System

Chapter Three will discuss using the DAD System in different capacities, whether you are a business using it with your employees, parents using it with your student-children, or a bunch of professionals forming a study group. If you are going to engage yourself in *The Growth Game*, on your own merit, then it is probably best to follow these steps to make sense of the development device.

Step One: Affirmations: Where do you want to grow?

You can use the system just to track the people you are meeting and the learning you are attaining on a daily basis as a planning resource. However, the system can help you the most when you have a few, specific long term goals or accomplishments that you care about. If you want to grow but you haven't thought about a few long term goals that you are passionate about, then this is the opportunity to do it. If you aren't passionate about a certain long term goal, then you probably will not care too much about developmental change.   What excites you? What are you driven by?   You will learn more about crafting affirmations or growth point statements later in the book.

Step Two: Awareness: First Gift of the Game

"People don't know, what they don't know." The DAD System will bring self-awareness to how much growth exposure you are having every day. Chances are, when you start to track what you are doing to develop yourself each day, you will realize a lack of growth in certain areas. The DAD System brings this awareness and allows you to change habits to grow, if you choose to do so.

Think of the DAD System as your scorecard in your own Growth Game. Much like starting a new workout or taking on a new sport, your weaknesses will quickly become evident after tracking your progress. In The Growth Game that weakness will be the areas of development that you are lacking exposure. If you have a "Shoot, I am not growing" moment, view it as the first gift of the game versus worrying about it. Awareness is the first step in affecting change.

Step Three: Actions and Activities Adjustment

After tracking your activities for a few days or weeks, reflect on what needs to change in order to achieve your longer term goals. What are the important action items that you need to execute? You may want to list significant shorter term benchmarks that will lead you to your longer term goal. "Before I achieve this…I must achieve this…"

With a few benchmarks in place, think about the learning and people that you need to acquire in order to give yourself the best chance of conquering the milestones and eventually attaining your long term goal. What type of people do you need to start to associate with? Who do you need to build better relationships with? What knowledge is necessary in order to achieve these goals or to build better connections with the people that you need to affiliate with?

Step Four: Accelerate

Up to this point, you have a clearer picture of the ways that you want to grow or long term goals that you want to achieve. You have also become aware of your current patterns and routine that you are accustomed to. With this information in view, you have game-planned the changes you need to make and mapped out shorter term benchmarks. In looking at these benchmarks you have given thought to the people you need to connect with and the learning you need to attain in order to give yourself the best chance of achievement. Now let's accelerate your growth through quantifying your commitments, which can lead to powerful mindset changes.

Use the DAD System to set a daily (or weekly) goal of how many points you need to acquire in order to feel as though you have made the most of your day (or week). When you achieve this amount, you know you gave the day your best shot and it was a productive step toward the longer term goal. The shorter-term assessment of your productivity can help with your mindset every day. If you achieved your daily point commitment, then that positive thought of accomplishment can birth positive feelings which usually equates to more positive and focused actions…this will compound into positive growth. If you did not hit your point commitment, and you did not make the most productive use of your day for your long-term goal or growth, then it should create more urgency to be more productive, focused, and driven in the following day.

If you just skipped over the first three steps and just try to quantify your day without connecting it to a longer term goal or growth opportunity that is important to you, then you will be less likely to follow through or even care. Why are you doing this?

Step Five: Accountability

No matter how self-motivated you are, having some type of additional accountability can greatly increase the chances that you follow through on your commitments. Join a professional or DAD study group, or share your reports periodically with someone who cares about your success. By doing this, you can get feedback, turn your growth into a game, and have competitions with other driven people based on scoring their development.

The system can be shaped to fit your personal or professional growth. You can shift the system's focus whenever you deem it necessary. The system serves as a framework to make each day more intentional and purposeful.   If you are laser-focused on a specific goal, you can make sure your points are dialed into meeting people and gaining learning that will specifically help you to achieve it.   If you do not have a specific project or venture you are looking to tackle, then you may want to treat the system with a more of a general approach. Using the system to build habits and track your activities will show you patterns of what your mind is absorbing and the type of people you are spending the time with. This will help you better understand the path you are on and help you make adjustments as you see fit.

-Chapter Two-

Score Keeping

A central focus of the DAD System is to quantify your exposure to growth for more purpose-driven days. It is a relative comparison and awareness system so that you can set goals and modify behavior in order to accelerate growth.

From week to week, the system allows you to diagnose your exposure to growth and analyze your patterns of point achievement. You will be tracking your life's short term input in order to change your long-term output. In this chapter, you will learn how to earn points.

The Z Points: Customized Values for Your Growth

Knowledge points in the DAD System are granted whenever you acquire relevant new knowledge that you internalized and would be able to convey to another

person, typically through reading, watching content, or learning from another person. Relationship builder points are earned by advancing a relationship with someone. Knowledge and relationship builders are considered Z points. Z is a customizable point value—you determine the value based on your comfort and discipline levels. A large component of growth is completing activities that do not come easily or naturally to you. Z points are customized to recognize this type of growth by awarding you a greater point value for activities that are outside of your comfort zone. The combination value of relationship builder points and knowledge points should equal three.

For example, an introverted bookworm would likely feel more comfortable achieving knowledge points versus relationship building points. Because the system is to promote growth, this person would customize his or her values to award only one point for knowledge attainment activities and two points for relationship builder activities. On the flip side, a socialite would be a natural at relationship building, but may not be as disciplined with solitary activities such as reading or studying. This person should customize his or her system to favor knowledge as the two-point play, and relationship builders as one point. A person who finds both activities equally easy or challenging should value both activities at 1.5 points.

The Categories

Affirmation Points

If you are part of an established business culture, you have probably heard about the book *Think and Grow Rich* by Napoleon Hill. The powerful book has practically become a business cliché. The book talks about the laws of attraction and our mind's process of creating what we feed it. Hill talks about his work with his mentor Andrew Carnegie, who believed that every human is given one thing in this world: control of his or her mind. The book also describes the habits of successful people. Hill theorized that the people who were most successful in their lives had a vision, articulated it, wrote it down, and revisited the vision regularly. Similar principles are discussed in other books like *The Science of Getting Rich* and *The Secret*.

Defining your success and training the brain to understand your goals is important to your growth. One way to do this is by crafting a vision statement. Vision statements have become mainstream in today's corporate and leadership worlds because of their effectiveness. Many successful people create a vision statement for a certain time point in the future. You may have different time framed vision statements, but five years is a good benchmark to start with. Take time to meditate on what you want your life to look like in five years. Anything that you desire personally and professionally should be written down. The more detailed you are, the more effective the statement will be. You should write the vision statement in present tense, as if you have already achieved what you want in the future. Use phrases that start with "I have" or "I am" instead of "I hope" or "I want." Keep your vision statement readily available and revisit it every day. Create a document and store it on your phone or email where you always can always access it. Reread it when you are waiting for appointments, after you wake up in the morning, and just before you go to bed at night.

After you create a vision statement, the DAD System rewards you every time you revisit your goals as part of your affirmation points. Award yourself one point every time you fully indulge in your vision statement or revisit a very specific goal. This helps you see the road ahead and drives your behavior toward your achieving those goals. Make it a habit. A good plan for you might be to wake up, brush your teeth, state your vision, and shower. Build it into your routine. Then at night, before bed, as you are tracking your points for the day, remind yourself to reaffirm.

Affirmations are one of the few DAD point values you can max out in a day. A best practice is to limit yourself to three affirmation points in a given day. Hill's book states that you should read a brief statement of success a dozen times a day, which you can certainly do, if you wish. However, remember development takes both vision and action. Having all your points coming from the affirmation category, all the time, could put you into a frustrating fantasy mentality.

Affirmations = 1 point

Best practice is to have a daily maximum of three points per day.

Definition: Spending time reflecting on, reading out loud or re-writing your vision, or meditating on a specific goal.

New Connection Points

New connections are a crucial part of achieving your goals. Every important person in your life right now— your employer, your spouse, your spiritual leader—all started with a new connection.

A new connection point is defined as being introduced to someone you have not previously met or interacted with. New connections include meeting a new co-worker, attending a networking event, or gaining a new referral. A new connection isn't a friend or even an acquaintance, but is a person you can contact on a favorable basis, because you exchanged contact information or share a mutual friend who has already made mention of you. Use your discretion if you run into someone whom you haven't talked to in years. This could be a "re-connection" point that would act in the same manner.

If you are not sure if your new connection qualifies, ask yourself these questions:

- Did I meet or introduce myself to someone new today?
- Do I know who they are and what line of work they are in?
- Do I know how we are connected or do we have a strong mutual acquaintance? Do I have their contact information?
- Do I intend on reaching out to this person in the near future?

If you can answer yes to all of those questions—then you have a new connection. You may wonder about connections you make through social media. Social media has made connecting with people second nature in our culture. People have Facebook friends they don't know or LinkedIn connections they have no clue about. Before you count these connections toward your DAD points, it may be best to test the validity of these connections.

When counting your social media connections toward your DAD points, be consistent. If you define your new connections liberally, understand it may take longer to build a relationship with that person or be more of a challenge to reach out to them if need be. If you hold yourself to a more conservative standard then you can be more confident in your true number of contacts.

New Connection = .5 point

Definition: Being introduced to someone you haven't met or talked to before.

You should know their profession, how you are connected to them and have their contact information. This could be a referral, an in person introduction or a virtual introduction.

Relationship Builders Points

I once worked with a new advisor who was a pretty good networker. She was always getting weakly introduced to people by way of referral or networking events. She knew the names of many people in the region and had a stack of business cards she had accrued from people in passing. This advisor eventually left the business because she never made more of all of these potential connections. Every time anyone would ask her about her business she would always say, "Slowwwwww. Planting seeds."

New connection points are your seeds and need the proper attention to grow. Anyone will give out a business card, shake your hand, or hit "Accept" on a social media invitation. But not all of those new connections will develop into a meaningful relationship. That is where relationship builder points come into play. Relationship builders are critical. They allow your connection seeds to blossom into meaningful contacts. They are important because they will showcase who you are spending time with. Behaviors, mindsets, and even income typically mirror the people you spend the most time with You may understand yourself at a deeper level if you can take a hard look at who you are spending the most time with.

Relationship builders are part of the Z points and have some degree of ambiguity. The first time you sit down for a cup of coffee to get to know someone, you are moving from a connection to a relationship. However, when you meet for the second or third time, those are relationship builders as well, as long as the relationship is strengthening on a personal level. Make sure you have an agenda or desired outcome for these relationship builder meetings. It does not and often shouldn't have to be a financial gain. Perhaps you want to learn more information about that person or get their perspective on a project you are working on.   Even if you do not get a deal or a transaction completed, if the relationship has advanced, the meeting would qualify for a relationship builder point.

Another way to gain some relationship builder points is to send a handwritten letter or card to people you haven't talked to in a while. How often do people get handwritten letters in the mail anymore? This is a great way to tell the people you have relationships with that you are thinking of them and it can be a powerful advancement for that relationship. A meaningful phone conversation would count as well.

As with the other Z point variable, knowledge, you want to figure out your Z point values before you start using your DAD System. If you don't know whether to give greater weight to your relationship builder points or knowledge points, ask someone who is close to you. If that doesn't give you clarity, chances are you fall right down the middle, and should value both at 1.5 points.

> Relationship Building = Z Score: 1 or 1.5 or 2
> point(s)
>
> Definition: An interaction with someone that advances or strengthens, at the very least, your personal relationship.

Meals

Numerous studies have shown the power of meals on reinforcing a relationship. Breaking bread with a person is an act that has brought people together since the beginning of time. The foundation of the Roman Catholic Church has its one billion followers coming together every Sunday to receive their God through the transubstantiation of unleavened bread.

If you have a meal with someone, you are almost forced to get to know them on a few levels throughout that 30-minute-plus period. The focus of meals is to get to know each other without distraction.

If you have a meeting in an office environment or at someone's home, the chances for distraction are imminent. Even if there are no interruptions by co-workers or family members, the person's environment calls their mind to other pressing issues besides the conversation at hand. When you meet in a conference room, your colleague will undoubtedly be distracted by their own familiar work environment. They may be thinking about the plants in the conference room that need to be watered, how there are never enough coasters for coffee mugs, or that they need to talk to that co-worker who walked right by the window. Going out for a meal, however, demands that person's undivided attention, free from the distractions of their familiar environments. Plus, meeting in this environment will make the interaction more memorable.

Another way to gather meal points is through an activity with another person. Play golf, go fishing, or go to an event. Even though the focus here may be on the activity instead of exclusively on the conversation at hand, chances are you are sharing adequate time with the person. Sharing an activity also brings you closer to the person.

Meal = 1 point

Definition: Sharing time with someone over a meal or meaningful event where their primary interaction is with you.

Note: Meal points would be in addition to the relationship builder, Z-point value.

Note: If you have a meal or participate in an activity with more than one person, the meal point would only be counted once.

Knowledge Points

Test scores and grades play a large role in all our lives from a young age. Our culture tells us that grades have a significant effect on a person's future and knowledge base. Students who have outstanding knowledge on a topic will be labeled as "A" students. These students are considered smart, will get into the best colleges, and will get the best jobs. Isn't that what we are taught?

Outside of your academic years, knowledge tends to be more practical. Mandatory industry tests and licensing requirements aside, most of the time you never fear an exam on the knowledge you accrue. But if a teacher isn't testing our knowledge, how do we know we are really learning at our maximum capacity?

Sometimes our thirst for knowledge is falsely quenched by mundane routines that provide us with our comfortable lifestyles. As long as we are somewhat comfortable with careers, lives, and ourselves, we tend not to focus energy on learning to expand our view of the world. This is a large mistake. The pursuit of knowledge allows us to dust off the lens with which we see the world through. It provides us with more insight on everything around us. The greater the scope of our knowledge, the easier it is for us to see the viewpoints of other people. When other viewpoints become clear, the opportunity opens for deeper connections. The more knowledge you have, the more value you bring to others.

If you were scheduled to meet with some representatives from Japan for a lucrative business deal, you would certainly prepare yourself for the meeting. You would read about their company, their products, their history, their culture and the way they conduct business so that you have the knowledge to connect deeper with the representatives. More than likely you have learned about this meeting ahead of time and had time to research and prepare. But we meet people every day who come from different cultures, lifestyles, and views. The more knowledge you have, the greater the chance of making an impactful connection with someone.

The good news is that technology has made it easy for us to learn anything about anything. There is no fun in asking trivia questions at a party, because your friends can Wikipedia the answer on their phone in two minutes. We are an information *now* society. I enjoy reading articles on my cell phone during my downtime or watching educational TED talk videos. It's amazing how much valuable content is on YouTube outside of the viral trash that gets passed around. There are many brilliant leaders and educators offering their wisdom and knowledge to anyone eager to listen. We can learn anytime, anywhere—it's just a matter of taking advantage of our resources.

If you could be an expert in one focused area, to get closer to your long term goals, what would you choose? What types of focused knowledge do you need to acquire?

Knowledge= Z score: 1 or 1.5 or 2 point(s)

Definition: Acquiring new, relevant knowledge that you can internalize and convey to someone else. The acquisition is typically through reading content, watching educational media or learning from another person.

Growth-Related Action and New Experiences

Possibly the most fulfilling category in the system are the new experience points. A new experience is anything you have done, completed, or lived through in which you took an action or asked someone to take action. Knowledge points allow you to say, "I know about that." New experiences allow you to say, "I've done that."

Growth-related or goal relevant actions (GRA) falls into the same category. This is executing an action that has significant impact on your development towards a longer term goal or general growth. This is an action that provides strong energy or excitement because you feel that you have grown or taken a momentous step toward an important goal.

New experiences can range from flying on a plane for the first time to flying to a new, exotic place. It could be your first public speech or getting fired. It could be the morning you hired your first employee, the night you went on a blind date, or that weekend you mourned the death of a close friend and tried an impressive scotch. You get the point. Pun intended.

Humans are creatures of habit. We wake up, eat, make money, eat, then go to bed. We can fall into a robotic lifestyle. New experiences, whether big or small, can get you off that treadmill.

Failures are powerful points that would count in this category. Losing a client, closing a business, and being rejected or fired are all strong forms of experiences. Although negative, they can help your development. Former Major League Baseball player Vernon Law said it best; "Experience is a hard teacher because she gives the test first, and the lesson afterwards."

Imagine that you are on your deathbed. Would you feel more at peace if you had a life full of different experiences instead of being on a constant treadmill? One of my most beloved family members is in his early seventies. He is not very wealthy and has suffered through the pain of losing many friends. But he has done so much in his life that I doubt he has many regrets. He is the type of guy who can hold a conversation about almost anything. If he doesn't have detailed knowledge on the topic, he probably is friendly with someone who does. He can always relate. I look at some other family members who are also smart, honest, and more financially sound, and they don't have the breadth of experience or relationship skills that he has. It seems as if they have lived on that constant treadmill for years and years.

Growth-related action is where the rubber can meet the road. You can have all the knowledge in the world and know hundreds of people, but it won't equate to anything unless there is a call to action.

Growth Related Action or New Experience
= 3 points

Definition: Participating or completing an activity that you have never done before or taking a significant action step toward completing a desired achievement.

Exposure with Action

DAD is a relative-comparative system based on the theory that the more aware you are of your short-term actions, the more control you have over your long term development. It cannot guarantee success. Therefore, there is no right or wrong amount of points for someone's growth. Acquiring 15 points in a day may be a goal for one professional that could yield the same positive, short-term reinforcement that eight points would for another professional.

Now that you know how to attain and track your points, it is important to understand that substantial growth requires action. The DAD System puts your growth exposure in front of your face so you can determine if you are giving yourself an opportunity to develop on a daily and weekly basis. It is a diagnostic tool that allows you to self prescribe where your energy should be spent. It is a game to play in order to bring a new passion to each morning and make the most out of the day.

High activity will present a world of opportunity to you but it will be up to you to capture it in the way that you wish. You can meet a bunch of people and learn a ton of information but if you are achievement driven, you will need to act on this exposure. Courage and persistence serve as the bridge between high opportunity and meaningful accomplishment. Be sure to keep an eye on courageous experiences and the persistence of your activities when trying to conquer a significant accomplishment.

This system is built for people who have an ambition to grow. Whether you are a student or a CEO, if you aren't looking to improve yourself, then you will not follow suit with the system. It is most beneficial if you play the game with someone else that can hold you accountable, or play in a contest with someone to see who can achieve the most points. This will allow you to be more proactive in your learning or relationship activities. There is obviously a certain level of ambiguity with the categories. If you are cheating on the amount of points, you are only cheating yourself. Chapter Three will cover the different capacities in which the DAD System can assist people and organizations in their growth.

-Chapter Three-

The Future Workforce

The DAD System will be able to help a variety of people and businesses at different stages. This chapter will discuss how the DAD System complies with businesses that are moving to a mobile workforce and Generation Y's behaviors. It will also look at how DAD can be powerful for students and how to conduct study group meetings from the tool.

Mobile Workforce

Some people call it working from home. I like to call it working from *phone*. Many white-collar professionals have the ability to work from home or any location that has Internet access. Not only does technology support this new workforce culture, but corporations and business owners are permitting and sometimes encouraging their workers to work remotely. Even the government is on board, passing their 2010 Tele-work bill that allows government employees to work remotely some days of the week.

In 2010, 24 percent of the country's workforce worked from home. That number will climb to over 33 percent by 2015, to 63 million workers. In a surveyed article on Payscale.com in March of 2012,[1] 66 percent of participants felt that their entire office could be "virtual" within five years. Of the 1,074 surveyed, 83 percent said they have spent at least part of their work week working from home in some type of capacity.

More and more managers and business owners will be okay with the workforce shift, as it can affect their bottom line in a few ways. In a 2012 article on BusinessWeek.com,[2] it is estimated that companies can save up to $8,000 per year per employee that works from home instead of in the office. Besides the savings, their employees will also be happier. Employees in the aforementioned Payscale.com article are cited as saying that they would give up other perks to work from home. Seventy-eight percent would give up free meals, 54 percent would give up their cell phone reimbursement, 31 percent would reduce their paid vacation and 25 percent would reduce salary.

---

[1] Payscale Human Capital
Brassfield, Margaret. March 2012. "Latest Telecommuting Statistics Reveal..." http://www.payscale.com/career-news/2012/03/working-from-home

[2] Bloomberg Business Week
Borenstein, Nathaniel. January 2012. "Forget the Office"
http://www.businessweek.com/debateroom/archives/2012/01/forget_the_office_let_employees_work_from_home.html

The higher up the position in the company, the more likely these professionals were spending time working from home.   These professionals usually aren't doing menial tasks.   Their work would fall into applying their learning, interacting with people, and making decisions. The bottom-of-the-totem-pole workers usually punch a clock and conduct redundant tasks.   The higher you climb up the hierarchal chart, the more the position becomes about interacting with people, while creating and sharing processes based on their learning and experiences. Most activities can be done from phone.   But how can the company capture and utilize all the daily activities of these professionals to use for building a culture and growing the organization?

A working-from-home business culture should create a happier workforce, which should lead to greater employee retention.   But you can already start to list the cons of this workforce shift.

Participants shared their three biggest issues with working from home as lack of direct communication, poor visibility into colleagues' activities, and reduction in data access.   This is where implementation of the DAD System can help in the culture shift.

Managers don't want to and will not be able to micromanage their workers in a work-from-home culture. Businesses will operate in a results-only environment. This could increase productivity, but innovation and culture may suffer.   The DAD System can bring transparency and a leverage effect to a workforce that goes virtual or remote.

Work-at-home employees should report two things to their company at the end of each day or week.   First, the results of whatever they are paid to work on, whether it is actual tasks or operations. But secondly, they should take two minutes a day or ten minutes a week and post their DAD report to appropriate parties inside their company. Transparency with the new contacts they made, who they spent time with, the things they learned, the experiences they had, and the goals they gave thought to serves as a culture cohesive that will be necessary.

Results-only work environments will falter because managers and colleagues will only know you by your results. The DAD report gives people insight on how they can leverage their learning and contacts for the greater good of the organization. A periodic conference call or in person meeting with each team member bringing in their DAD report for reflection will be the organization glue. This will allow for a compounding effect of the personnel's knowledge and relationships. Not to mention, it could add elements of fun and competition based on front-end activity using a point system.

The team-based DAD conference calls would allow remote professionals to share highlights of the people that they are meeting or experiences they are having. These are conversations that we may take for granted in a traditional working environment.

For example, take two professionals, Jack and Jill, who had offices next to each other at their firm and would always interact with each other throughout the day and constantly share information, even if they didn't realize they were doing it. Now their company shifts to a work-from-home culture and only requires them to be in the office for meetings one day a week.

Both Jack and Jill spend hours working from home trying to connect with prospective clients for their firm or perhaps even researching information for a creative project they were working on. Jack has been trying all week to get introduced to a vice-president at ABC Corporation and he has had no luck. Jill, on the other hand, attended a charity event this week in which the same vice president at ABC Corporation also volunteers. Having Jill report her DAD points and activities to her team members, or posting them for review will allow more transparency in a work-from-home environment. This could even be beneficial in a traditional working environment. Jack would then be able to get introduced to the person he was looking to meet, all because of a DAD team conference call. The same effect would occur for leveraging learning.

The other potential pitfall with a shift to a mobile workforce is that most positions become "results only." This isn't necessarily a bad thing at face value. Team members can work at home and do whatever they wish as long as the results are there.   Besides losing the transparency and leverage effect that we shared in the Jack and Jill example, it can also disconnect the company culture.   There is the danger that employees or team members are only seen as laborers and relationships with their co-workers are purely transactional, stat-driven or results based. We only look at their output and don't reflect on dissecting their input.   Relationships that managers will have with their team members will start to become superficial. But if the manager could receive a DAD report (daily or weekly), he could have more meaningful conversations with his team members and look to more effectively coach them based on their daily activities that don't show up on the company's results report. Plus it will give an "end point" to the day for team members or employees working from home. Instead of punching a clock, they take two minutes to post their DAD reports, reflect on their points and what they accomplished during their day, and then adjust to leisure or family time.

Generation Y Make Up

Generation Y or the Millennials (born in early 1980s to late 1990s depending on who you ask), make up 25 percent of the workforce in 2013 and will make up 75 percent of the workforce by 2025. This generation was babysat by video games, has *seen* a lack of commitment due to the divorce rates and corporate layoffs of their parents, and they have been pampered with trophies for coming in 9th place in competitions. This all can have an influence on the future workforce.

Millennials are most prone to delayed gratification issues. They are accustomed to always knowing what their friends and family members are doing via social media. They are also accustomed to having access to information within a few clicks of a mouse or with buttons on a phone. It is part of their every day, but how often is Gen Y harnessing, quantifying and effectively using this storm of information and connections to be useful in planning their future?   How are they recalling all the data and connections they have taken in and use it for personal or professional growth in the future?   The DAD System allows Gen- Y to hit short-term, daily goals to aid in the delayed gratification.   It permits them to answer the questions, "Did I do everything I could possibly do today?" and then be scored.   Only the ambitious will comply.

Gen Yers are fickle. A 2012 Chicago Tribune article[3] cited that Gen Yers will change jobs every three years. Using the DAD System for their own professional development will allow Millennials to recall and showcase all the experiences, learning, and relationships they have from past careers to help them in their future career, all in one place. A DAD report could serve as a complement to the traditional resume as well. Wouldn't it be powerful to have the ability to show future employers all the learning, experiences, and relationships that you have had instead of just putting your former company and title on a piece of paper?

If you aren't looking to change jobs but would like to try to improve yourself every day, Generation Y could have a Growth Game contest with each other. The DAD System allows you and your friends to challenge each other to concentrate on your professional development in a fun and competitive way.   Users can post their daily point totals to their social media networks.

Ownership and Gen Y Employees

We have all seen how corporations were quick to switch their branding and marketing to appeal to Gen Y customers.   But how are they changing their internal

[3] Chicago Tribune (from web)
    Samuelson, Kristin. February 2012. "Retaining Gen Y Employees" http://articles.chicagotribune.com/2012-02-05/business/ct-biz-0205-outside-opinion-gen-y-20120205_1_baby-boomers-workplace-generation-x-employees

development systems to grow their Gen-Y workforce?

As in any research on an entire generation from all different walks of life, there will be conflicting theories and information. Is Gen-Y ambitious or are they lazy? Are they entrepreneurial or are they risk-averse? It is impossible to properly label this entire generation outside of the fact that they have grown up in a technology revolution.

The most important word in managing and leading a Gen Y professional is ownership. It's not so much about what these employees need to do to move up the conventional chain and earn more money like past generations. It's more about: what is the employee doing that they have a very high level of input and responsibility for now? And how does this experience not only connect to the greater good of a purpose driven organization, but how can the employee spin off into another ownership role either inside or outside of your company? Many Millennials care more about the appearance of winning than feeling the actual emotion of accomplishment. Simply put, how can this role possibly help their individual brand?

Many corporations are turning to "game-ification' for their sales forces to have more fun and recognition in sales competitions. This will be an effective sales motivator for Gen Y. The DAD System is intended to act as a universal language or measuring stick, across all professions, for people to track their development activities. The system is something they can take with them throughout all career changes and throughout their evolving lives.

Students

It seems like the family dinner at the end of the day is a fading tradition. The days where a family of four sits down at the dinner table, with the television and cell phones off, discussing their days are few and far between. I don't believe anything will replace that family interaction time. But the DAD System can be a passive way for driven and busy high school students to log in their daily activities for both parents and career counselors to use for development purposes. If parents use the system as well for their own professional careers, it can create a fun, growth-oriented competition for the family. It is more of an engaging way for everyone in the family to help each other and understand what goes on in their lives throughout the day versus the boring, "How was your day?" conversations.

I wish I had created the DAD System while I was in college. I wish I could recall what every week looked like during those development years. It would have been beneficial for me to revisit key concepts that I learned in class or experiences I had that I could go back to now with more life experience and maybe a greater appreciation for. Never mind being able to recall all the people I met. Yes, social media sites assist in keeping in touch, but most people have a hard time making the contacts intentional or purposeful. Not to mention just having an awareness of my daily activities while preparing for the real world. There is an opportunity for college career advisors to use the DAD System to help coach their students to best prepare them to enter the career they want. And for students to recondition themselves to have purpose-driven days from the day they step foot on campus. They can capture their college experiences for later reflection and use throughout their lives by posting their activities at the end of each day or week.

Buddy System

The DAD System will work best when the users have some accountability. Playing the Growth Game with a sibling, a friend, or a co-worker can be valuable motivation. Much like the buddy system helps us to lose weight, quit smoking, or stick with an exercise program, a Growth Game partner will help you get into the habit of using the program. Make it fun and challenge each other to grow.

Let's assume, in your life right now, that it is six o'clock in the evening and your cell phone is ringing. You look down and see your best friend's name on your caller ID. You answer and start the conversation.

You: What's going on, Mike?

Mike: Not too much, how was your day?

You: Okay. You?

Mike: My day was good. Want to play golf tomorrow?

You: Sure. Make the tee-time and I will see you at the course around 3pm.

If you and Mike were playing the Growth Game together, we would eliminate the ambiguous "good, bad and okay" days. You answer the phone:

You: What's going on, Mike?

Mike: Wrapping up my day. I am at 7 points, you?

You: I'm at 10. I met 12 new people at that seminar today that you told me about. Your idea worked.

Mike: Congrats on the 10 point day. I was going to put off reading those research articles until after the weekend but I might do it tonight to try to catch up to you. Do you want to play golf tomorrow?

You: Sure. Make the tee-time and I will see you at the course around 3pm. I'll ask you about those articles.

Multiplier Meetings and Study Groups

Are you part of a professional development study group right now? A monthly check-in meeting or call with other people using the system will help you receive objective feedback, learn from each other's new experiences and knowledge, and help you build relationships with each other. These groups serve as a multiplier effect to your growth exposure, therefore the term multiplier meetings. This can help whether you are a small business using DAD for employee development, or if there are a bunch of individuals in different professions coming together for a self-improvement study group.

The first benefit of multiplier meetings is that you gain an outside perspective on your growth patterns while everyone is speaking a similar language. Even though DAD can be a great self-monitoring system, there will always be bias. It is good to have someone question why you have lunch three times a week with one specific person or ask why you haven't had a new experience in weeks. By having people look at your reports, they can challenge you and pick up on things that you may not see. They bring caring accountability.

Second, you can expand your knowledge through your peers. You'll learn about their most important findings and teachings through the books they read or videos they have watched. You will also learn from their experiences, which could be invaluable.

Third, if you are very close to your group you can share contacts and connections that you have met over the past month to aid each other's growth. This can be great with a group of small business owners in a local community.

The agenda for a multiplier meeting:

1. Report points and review commitments

2. Get feedback from the group

3. Leverage learning and people

4. New commitments

Share your DAD sheet in person or electronically with the group. To start the meeting, each person should state how many points he or she committed to from last time and how many they actually received. Whoever had the most points should get their "face time" first.

A member would start off by reflecting on the points they achieved in each category and report to the group if they achieved their commitments from last month. The member would also take a few minutes to share what went on in each category. For example, sharing where they felt they had the most growth or what they struggled with the most.

The study group may make some observations and share feedback based on the numbers of the report. Some sample questions group members could ask include:

- We can see where you are achieving the most points, where is the most energy spent?
- What got in the way of hitting your commitments from last month?
- Why are you getting lunch with Bob Smith four times a week?
- Where did the majority of the connections come from?
- Why did you only have two new experience points throughout the entire month?
- What is getting in the way of revisiting your affirmations frequently?

The member can then share what piece of learning or interaction was the most powerful throughout the month. This can elicit more feedback but is intended to educate or help the group learn from your month of activities. This can be leveraging ideas, knowledge, or contacts. In wrapping up each member's face time, they should commit to both a point commitment goal (either in total or in a specific category) and share what their focus will be throughout the upcoming month. Then you would continue with the next member getting his or her face time.

You can build the study groups with your friends or colleagues. It may be more beneficial to build them with a variety of professionals in the area or with similar professionals throughout the country. These groups can be a remarkable instrument in your development, especially if you work for yourself or do not have many active mentors.

Section Two

➕➕

Internal Development

"We cannot teach people anything; we can
only help them discover it within
themselves"- Galileo

Now that you have a general overview of the DAD
System, Section Two explores your internal
development—the ways you change through the activites
of affirmations, new experiences, and knowledge. The
ways you grow internally and your relationships with
others are interdependent. Through visioning, knowledge,
and new experiences, you will meet new people who will
provide you with opportunities to encounter new
experiences, gain more knowledge, and shape life into your
vision.

Affirmation, knowledge, and new experience points
are under your control. You control writing down your
goals and your vision statement. Scheduling time to learn

new knowledge is also up to you. In most circumstances, new experiences or growth-related actions are in your control as well. Your internal development should have little reliance on other people— just you, yourself and your mind.

Chapter Four will help you stop thinking about goals as end results and will bring urgency to your affirmations. Chapter Five introduces you to your EGA—extreme growth alarm—and shows you how to coach yourself through nerve-racking new experiences that change the trajectory of your development. Chapter Six explains the importance of training your mind to effectively download and internalize necessary knowledge in an information infested world.

-Chapter Four-

Affirmations to Activities

Most people believe that goals are important to success. Simply having goals is often an indicator that a person wants to grow. The definition of a goal is the result or achievement toward which effort is directed; an aim, an end. The definition has the word 'end' in it. Meaningful goals take work and discipline to achieve. However, achieving the goal shouldn't be viewed as an end point. In fact, it is usually a new beginning. Goals breed more opportunity for growth.

We are told at a young age to dream big. But very few of us have a process around formulating goals and using them to drive our behavior. If more professionals viewed goal planning as an art form versus an emotionally detached formality, they would be more apt to achieve them. How do your goals actually drive your behavior? What process do you use in formulating goals?

Let's use the goal of "running a successful business" for our example. A novice goal setter would simply say:

My goal is to run a successful business.

The first problem here is that the goal it too vague and isn't measurable. Any professional consultant will tell you that your goals should be measurable. What is a measurement that gets you highly energized over the goal? A veteran goal setter would apply a measurement and deadline:

My goal is to run a business that generates $1,000,000 of revenue in three years.

If you reviewed this goal, either by rereading it or saying it out loud every day, as stated, it may not be viewed as an end point. But it certainly doesn't take into consideration opportunities that will stem from the achievement. It also doesn't help you reflect on your needed behavioral changes. Let's rework that measurable goal into a growth point process where the end goal seems to be placed into a natural progression of actions and behaviors, and breeds other opportunities after achievement. The process is as follows:

Growth Point Process

1. Craft "Growth Point" affirmation language and reflect on it frequently
2. Bring your future mindset forward to the present
3. Align activities

After you have declared a goal that you are passionate about, made it measurable, and have stamped a deadline to accomplish it, you can then transform it into a growth point. The first step in putting it into a growth point process is to rework your affirmation language to place the goal into a natural progression of your life. Look at your next passionate goal as a springboard into a life of further growth opportunities. Write your growth points in the present tense and as detailed as possible, as if you have already accomplished them. Then reflect on being in that state and see what opportunities would be available to you then.

Three Years From Today

I have a business that generates $1,000,000 of revenue. We were recognized as one of the fastest growing companies in the metro area based on sales. We have three talented employees so that I can concentrate on more strategic planning. We have helped over 500 clients in this brief time period and have built some buzz through smedia outlets such as the Journal Ledger and KABC television. We have given back to three of our favorite charities over the past year and were a gold sponsor at the Metro Half Marathon for cancer awareness...

Then Reflect:

Now that I have achieved this goal, the opportunities that are now available to me:_____

Now that I have achieved this goal, my mindset has changed in that:

_____

Remember that there will be plenty of opportunities that are going to be available to you that you currently aren't even aware of. What else could create more excitement and urgency around an accomplishment than not knowing what you are currently missing out on or are impervious to?

After you have meditated on what the achievement can offer you in terms of a future line of opportunity, you need to start reconditioning your mindset. The first reconditioning process is to frequently revisit your growth points. Make a habit of reading or rewriting these goals. These would be affirmation points in your DAD System. The DAD System will allow you to view periodically, how much time you are dedicating towards training your brain to internalize these goals.

After you are in the habit of reflecting on your goals, you can start to recondition your behaviors in a certain way. Start to bring the future mindset that you will possess after accomplishing the growth point to the present. There is a saying, "dress for the job you want, not the one you have." Attempt to do that with your mindset. Think as if you are in the position you want versus the current position you are in. How does your behavior change?

It might be a challenge to acquire this mindset even though we are in complete control of our thoughts. No one can tell you how you can think. Just because you don't have a business that generates $1,000,000 of revenue yet, doesn't mean you cannot attempt to think like someone who does.

How can you change your perspective and attitude? What would be different and what experience would you have to help mold your thinking? So ask yourself, "How does someone that has already achieved a goal similar to this, think and act differently than me?" If you don't know, try to study people or ask the people that have already achieved the goal you are striving for.

Action ignites attitude. Once you have committed to start thinking in a different way, feed the reconditioning process through action. This is where you can use the DAD System to help you.

Aside from affirmation points, you can monitor your

knowledge and new experiences to help cast the mindset you need to develop. Start reading the books or journals that the people you aspire to be like would read. Start acting on new experiences. Try new things that you think you would be more apt to try if you had already accomplished the goal. Use your DAD System to monitor the contacts you are making and the people you are spending time with. Do you want to develop a mindset like the people you are spending the most time with or should you become involved with other social spheres?

Use the DAD System to see if the activities you conduct everyday are helping or hindering you from the growth point you are pursuing. Come up with an activity plan that aligns your DAD points with the tasks that are necessary to achieve your next growth point. Affirmations are the easiest points to receive in the DAD System because they are entirely up to you. Are you carving out time to reflect on your future goals?

Once you stack a few different growth point affirmation statements together, you will be forming your vision statement. Share these with people close to you. Then start to work backwards to the present; to the things you need to learn, the people you need to meet, and the tasks you need to complete to put you closer to attainment. Think big, start small, act now.

Exercises:

Take a certain goal you have now and state it:

Why is that goal important to you now?

How will you measure achievement of this goal?

When must you complete it by?

How will achieving that "growth point" affect your mindset?

In what ways can you possess the mindset now, before you achieve it?

What other opportunities may come from achieving that growth point?

When I achieve _____,   _____ will be available to me.

Now rework your affirmation language in the present tense and store it somewhere where it is easily accessible. Who should you share these growth points with? What learning must you acquire or what people do you need to meet and build relationships with in order to accelerate you through this growth point? Start vague and then dial it down to be more specific.

In order to achieve my next milestone, I must gain more learning in _____. I must connect deeper with people in_____.

Then commit to a certain amount of "focused" points that will accelerate your exposure towards the goal. Focused points are points that are very specific to the goal at hand. These would be included in your overall points for the day, but are more purposeful and meaningful.

- I commit to attain _____ focused new connection points every _____ until I _____.

- I commit to attain _____ focused relationship builders points every _____ until I _____.

- I commit to attain _____ focused meal points every _____ until I _____.

- I commit to attain _____ focused knowledge points every _____ until I_____.

- I commit to attain _____ focused GRA- new experiences points every _____ until I_____.

- I commit to reviewing my focused affirmations _____ times every _____until I_____.

I will be accountable to not only myself and my future but also an accountability partner or team mate. This external accountability will come from _____ and we will reflect on my DAD report every _____. If I do/do not achieve _____ then I will/ will not _____.

Point-Based vs. Time-Based Planning

The DAD System could be a substitute for your time commitment towards a project or start up business. Many entrepreneurs may say they will give their business a solid try for a set period of time. Instead of committing to an opportunity or business for say, one year, you could instead commit to the amount of DAD points you must acquire, totally focused on the business, before you can quit. In financial services, great new advisors aren't products of time, they are products of *times*. Meaning if you have been in business for three years and have 100 clients or been in business for 1 year and have 100 clients, you have the same amount of experience.

The DAD System can allow you to commit to a new business or start a new career in terms of your exposure to growth versus a time commitment.

"If I can have 300 new experience points (100 new experiences from this business) or 100 new connection points (met 200 new people), then I will allow myself to re-evaluate my business at that time".

Your commitment is now an exposure race that will have ancillary benefits versus hanging around in a business until a certain date on the calendar. What's more effective? Starting a business and telling yourself to give it a year and you mess around half the time because you are already checked out? Or say, "once I have acquired 200 relationship building points with 200 knowledge points from the business, then I will evaluate if I want to continue." If you can do this in six months, it was probably more impactful then just saying, "I'll evaluate my business in a year."

By using the DAD System in this way, you guarantee your *exposure* to growth. If the business or venture goes as planned, then you have grown. If you decide the new venture or career isn't for you, at least you have evidence of the people you met and the things you learned along the way. Documenting this allows you to share the contacts and knowledge you have gained with your future business partner, employer, etc., versus just adding another line on your resume.

-Chapter Five-

Silencing Your EGA

It's five minutes before you are set to take the stage to conduct a presentation for over 500 people in your company. The speaker before you is wrapping up his talk with a punch line that brings home his whole speech. People are laughing. He nailed it. You are prepared, but you have never presented to an audience this large or accomplished. It also doesn't help that the speaker before you was flawless. You feel anxious and your stomach is turning. That's simply your EGA starting to go off.

Your *Extreme Growth Alarm* (EGA) drags you from comfort into an abrupt stage of growth. It rings any time you feel nervous, scared, or apprehensive about a new or uncomfortable situation. It often is alerting and challenging your Ego, which by philosophical definition is the conscious element that knows experience. If your EGA had a voice it would chant, "Warning, you are leaving your comfort zone. Growth ahead!"

When you feel your EGA going off recognize it as a

growth opportunity to embrace rather than a discomfort you should fear. Even if you do not get what you want out of the experience, you probably will learn and grow from it.

Look at your EGA as if you are "capturing your butterflies." When we were kids, our parents referred to a case of nerves as having butterflies in our stomachs. All of these nerve-racking moments gave us growth. The first day of school, leaving your home for the day, leaving your parents, taking your first test, or asking someone out on a date are all growth points. Sometimes we let these butterflies fly away from us, and run away from the uncomfortable situation. We'd rather stay like a caterpillar in our comfort cocoon. But every time we fail to capture our butterflies, we let a new experience escape us.

How many times did your EGA go off in the past month? How many times did you hit snooze on your EGA and delay the growth opportunity? How many butterflies did you capture in the past week? How many did you let get away?

When your EGA rings

Your EGA will probably ring most frequently with new experiences. We can certainly grow from reading books, watching educational videos, and meeting people, but handling a new or uncomfortable experience or taking action on a relevant goal can instantly impact your growth. You probably don't get that feeling of butterflies when you read a book and grow through a typical intake of knowledge. This is why A+ students in school aren't always the best leaders in the real world. They are disciplined to studying or can absorb knowledge easily, but they might not be able to manage their EGA effectively or have faltered upon taking growth-related action.

Now that you know what your EGA is, let's talk about some processes to effectively handle it and allow yourself to be OPENN to growth.

1. One Hundred Percent Mentality
2. Preparation
3. Enthusiasm
4. Negotiate Negativity
5. Notes

One Hundred Percent -Win-Win Outcomes

When your EGA goes off, tell yourself that regardless of outcome, you will grow. Having this win-win mentality will make it easier to step out of your comfort zone. Steven Covey talks about win-win in terms of problem solving in his legendary book, *Seven Habits of Highly Effective People*. When your EGA rings, think of every outcome as a winning situation.

Some financial professionals use a win-win proposition to approach the role of the phone. Advisors are taught that the entire goal of a phone call is to get an appointment with a prospective client. If the prospective client said "no", as they did half of the time, the advisor feels like he or she is losing 50 percent of the time. Some advisors played a psychological trick on themselves and said that the goal of a phone call should instead be to determine if that client is a right fit for you. Regardless of whether the answer was an acceptance or a rejection, the advisor still wins, because he or she met this goal. Use this win-win thinking for your own EGA moments. How can you recreate win-win scenarios for the tasks that set your EGA off?

Preparation

In most extreme growth experiences, you will have time to prepare. There are always unforeseen fight-or-flight reactionary experiences, like when you see a bad car accident and you need to help the injured people. But in most professional and personal development cases, you will have time to think and compose a plan. Preparation is a main key to silencing the volume of your EGA.

Prior Planning Prevents Poor Performance.

The less you plan, the greater the chance of having a poor performance. If you've had a lot of poor performances, you'll be reluctant to tackle your EGA the next time it rings.

Aside from task preparation, you can prepare for EGA situations by learning more about yourself. Months before writing this book, I went through a number of personal assessments that tested anything from my leadership strengths to my selling styles. I did about five different personal assessments, some more in depth than others, all within a two-month period. It allowed me to really understand the lens with which I see the world through. Knowing as much as possible about yourself— how you react, your strengths and weaknesses, and your viewpoints— will help you be prepared for all types of growth situations when you do not have time to prepare.

Enthusiasm

Enthusiasm is a powerful tool. Enthusiasm comes from the Greek, "En Theos" which means "god within". All Supreme Beings in religions want their creations to grow, and doing things with enthusiasm eases the process. When your EGA goes off, instead of feeling anxious, feel enthusiastic that you have another opportunity to grow. Think to yourself, "I am fortunate that I get an obvious chance to grow today." Enthusiasm is just a second cousin to anxiety. Both are degrees of excitement, but enthusiasm is much more fun to be around.

Your EGA only goes off inside of you, but you may broadcast it to everyone through your body language and tone. No one needs to know that your EGA is going off. Show enthusiasm even if you have to fake it. Sales professionals always talk about faking your confidence until you have it. Substitute your anxiety with enthusiasm. It can help to disguise your uneasiness and open up your mind to being more receptive to the positive effects of the experience.

Negotiate the Negativity

Your EGA comes with a battery—fear. Fear only exists in your mind. A little fear is good for you. We wouldn't know when we are growing if we didn't have fear. Too often, however, we let the F-word take over and grasp at our decision making abilities.

The strongest EGA will go off when you are doing something you have never done before. You need to reposition this fear as a positive emotion instead of a crippling one. View fear as a friend who cares about you but has a very weird way of showing it. It's the friend who wants you to live a more fulfilling life but wants to make sure you are ready for it.

When your EGA goes off, your current stage of development is negotiating with your future development. Your current life is challenged by a newer, more experienced you. You are upgrading yourself. Ask yourself these questions and then charge forward:

"I may not know what the exact outcome of this situation is going to be, but will I let a feeling created in my own mind prevent me from finding out?"

"Will I let temporary anxiety prevent me from receiving lifetime experience?"

"Is being comfortable more important than getting better?"

"This is growth. Do you want to grow?"

"Am I being a wimp right now?   How many very successful wimps do I know?"

"Will I regret inaction? What am I giving up today?"

"Am I being a leader? What would (role-model) do?"

"Will avoiding this situation now cause a damage control situation in the future?"

"Will I be respected by inaction?   Will I respect my decision of inaction?"

Notes

EGA experiences typically involve interacting with other people. More specifically, most EGA experiences occur because of your apprehensions of how others will perceive you. After going through an experience that sets your EGA blaring, go back to the people who saw you grow and ask for their feedback. Even if you didn't accomplish the outcome you desired, the instruction and feedback will be part of a winning experience. In most cases, it will also strengthen the relationship with these people as well.

Do the Right Thing

Courage is really a form of caring. When your EGA rings, you will know the right thing to do, even if it's not the easiest. Think back to your school days when you saw someone being teased.   We all knew the right thing to do was to stand up for that person, but our EGA often got in the way. If you did stand up for the person, you were growing as a leader.

I could always get a taste of someone's true character when they were leaving the financial services business. On a few occasions I knew a professional was struggling, yet I still respected them for their integrity and determination. Nothing would put a black mark on their name faster than when we walked in Monday morning and their cube was totally cleared off. It was easier for them to pack their stuff over the weekend when no one was in the office and leave, than approach the managing partner about their decision. Often times, the managing partner would have assisted them in finding their next career opportunity. A ten-minute, honest conversation was too hard, so they took the easy way out. The temporary discomfort of the EGA prevented the continuance of a relationship and possible future benefits down the road.

I was even taken aback by people who wouldn't even say "thank you" when given an opportunity with the firm. I was astonished at the number of Generation Y-ers and even Generation X-ers that fell off the face of the planet instead of saying, "Thank you, but I decided on a different path."   If there was ever a remote chance you were going to say "yes please" to an opportunity, make sure you decline politely with "No thank you, but I appreciate the consideration" if you decide not to pursue it further.

Generation Y is prone to doing the wrong thing when it comes to delivering important messages or dealing with conflict management. Instead of doing the right thing with a phone call or a face to face conversation, depending on the topic, they send an email or text.

The EGA is your most important development muscle.   Like most muscles in your body, the more you use it, the stronger it will become. There is a tendency to shy away from these types of extreme growth circumstances, so be proactive and look for opportunities that will challenge your comfort zone and simultaneously train your EGA.

-Chapter Six-

Information Epidemic

Learn in all ways, always.   Learn from reading, television, your computer, your phone, and other people. Information has never been as accessible as it is today and it is only going to become easier to obtain in the future. If you have a question, you probably could get the answer within two minutes. If you can't sit still to read an entire book, you could watch a YouTube video highlighting the main points. You can get a college degree online. Efficient transfer of information is the purpose of technology.

The knowledge points in the DAD System stem from the Learning Law of Readiness stated by Professor Edward Thorndike in the early 1900s. This law states that when you see the value in learning, you will be more receptive to information. You were probably more enthused by your elective courses in college versus the mandatory courses you didn't want to take. The DAD

System gives you a particular objective to learning; the knowledge will help you grow. You can easily tell yourself, "I want to read this book because it will help me grow towards an achievement." Or, "I am ready to watch this video series because it will help me grow into a well rounded person." This knowledge is positively reinforced through points.

Some people monitor their checking account like a hawk. Others monitor the calories and carbohydrates they eat. But how often do we habitually monitor what we feed our minds? The DAD System allows you to monitor the types of information you consume. There is an epidemic of information available to us—it's up to us to use it for our benefit. It may help to start implementing a systematic way to effectively process and internalize all the information that is out there.

Absorb Now

If you have the opportunity to learn now or later, choose now. There is a benefit to taking in knowledge at this very moment versus delaying it by even a few hours.

We don't know what we don't know. We constantly see the world through our current learning lens made up of our knowledge and our experiences. The more learning we acquire, the wider that lens becomes. Think back to your childhood, when you put an empty paper towel roll over your eye as if it were a scope. You'd lose all of your peripheral vision and could only see a few objects at a time. With every bit of knowledge you download to your mind, you expand the width of that paper towel roll. You see things more objectively. The more knowledge you internalize, the more opportunity you have to learn more, meet more people, and grow faster. Obtaining information now can help you see the world clearer in an hour.

You have to make choices in terms of the types of

knowledge you want to absorb.   Often times you cannot just put life on hold to digest knowledge. However, if you have the time to read an article or watch a video free of distractions immediately, don't put it off. The information you obtain might help you in the next conversation you have. Eleanor Roosevelt is often attributed to saying, "Great minds discuss ideas. Average minds discuss events. Small minds discuss people."   Without the continuous updating of knowledge it is difficult to discuss stimulating ideas.

Drain Out Bias

With so many different resources for information today, we must add an extra step in our learning process. When we listen to a pitch from a salesman or a stance on a debatable issue from a politician we can easily identify their bias. But what about the bias that comes from all the little pieces of information you take in on a daily basis? We are well into the information age and there is a ton of recycled data that has been "spun". After you get in the habit of acquiring more relevant knowledge, make sure you have a process to drain out bias.

Bias can be blatant or subtle. Financial and political bias can be blatant. If you read a book, watch a video clip, or even have a conversation with someone, it is always good to find how where their bread is buttered, or how they make their money.

The more subtle types of bias that you may have to drain out of the information you absorb are cultural, religious, geographical, age, timing, and educational bias. The more you can learn about the creator's background, the easier it will be to identify potential bias. You could read a book or journal by two brilliant Harvard professors on the same exact topic. But perhaps one author is 35 years old and the other is 65 years old. Will that have any effect on the way they convey the message in their book? Or one author grew up in Tokyo and the other in rural Nebraska. It might not affect the core of the information but maybe the tone or slant is which the information is positioned.

Another example is if you watch two different television interviews about the economy and the future job markets.   One interviewee just learned that his job is in question due to potential company layoffs.   The other interviewee found out that his company is hiring ten more people in his department alone.   Even though they have access to the same economic research and their companies may not have a great effect on the economy at a macro level, their personal lives can spin their message or delivery.

Immediate gratification can get in the way of acquiring proper knowledge as well. We tend to fall victim to a "page one" mentality when doing research on the Internet. Meaning we don't look much further than the results on the first few pages of a Google search. According to Optify, a digital marketing software company, being the first result on the first page of a Google search will result in a 36 percent chance of being "clicked." Being on the first page only gives you a 8.9 percent chance, and if your site is on page two of a search, there is only a 1.5 percent chance it will get clicked on in a search.   Impressive search engine optimization doesn't always translate into the most accurate and beneficial information. The exercise of draining out bias from information is not intended for you to become a complete skeptic. It is intended to help you, your mind, and your outlook be strengthened through pure knowledge and your own thought.

Internalize

After you drain out the bias, the new information needs to be internalized before it becomes valuable. I would frequently witness brand new financial professionals learn about a tax code or research from a veteran advisor and then they would try to implement it immediately. It sounded brilliant to them, so they attempt to use it right away. They didn't give proper time to internalize it. When your mind isn't accustomed to taking in valuable information, new knowledge can act as poison. This poison causes you to blurt out what you just learned to everyone even though it may have no relevance. We all know someone who read an intelligent article in a newspaper that morning and then worked it into a conversation with everyone they talked to that day, as if it was their own thought.

I've noticed an interesting comparison between the advisors who came into the business with many contacts and those who had a limited network. The majority of the time, the advisor with a large circle of contacts would have at least a small amount of knowledge on an array of different topics. Whether it was current events, sports, technology, geography, history, lifestyle, or pop culture, they would be a good choice to have on a Trivial Pursuit team, even if their deeper knowledge on these topics was limited. The advisors who came into the business with limited connections had a harder time meeting new people. These advisors could have deep discussions with certain areas of interest, but often had only a few topics in which they could converse.

Many business and social media experts will argue that specialization is crucial in the digital world. You need to be an expert on something. I agree that you should have expertise in a certain area and brand yourself towards that niche. Being the go-to source on one particular topic will attract people. After you have conquered your niche though, challenge yourself to receive knowledge points learning about different markets, topics, or areas of interest to see how your focus can be positioned in areas where you are not well versed. By having a broader base knowledge lens, you will be able to have better connections with the people who are gravitating toward your expertise. Knowledge is power but many careers rely more on the practice of human understanding. Section Three will show you proactive ways to build your network of contacts and how to give yourself the best chance of forming better relationships.

Instructions for Proper Knowledge Digestion:

1. Absorb frequently: Through reading, watching content or personal instruction.

2. Drain out the bias:

   Everyone has a bias. It could be financial, geographical, cultural, corporate, religious, political, educational, or timing/age bias.

   When people share knowledge, it is tainted with bias.
   a. What bias may the creator of the content or source have?
   b. How is your bias affecting the way you are learning this information?
   c. Research other angles
   d. What bias might you give when you pass it on?

3. Internalize:
   a. Let the knowledge simmer before relaying it.
   b. Articulate the main points in your own words. See if you can paraphrase the key concepts of what you learned.
   c. Ask yourself, "Can I educate someone else on the matter?"

    d.   Objectivity comes from stating what your potential bias is when communicating

4.   Use where applicable

Section Three

✚ ✚ ✚

People

"I don't deal with companies, I deal with people within companies. No set of buildings ever provided me with referrals, more work, or support."- Alan Weiss, World Consulting Expert

No matter which field you are in, you need people. The greatest actor in the world won't get anywhere unless he networks to find the right agents and producers. You can create the most practical invention, but what good is it if you cannot put it in front of an audience? The greatest basketball player in the world remains undiscovered if he does not get scouted. Almost every successful person will realize that if it wasn't for meeting and connecting with other people, they wouldn't be in the position they are today.

As we have discussed in previous chapters, technology has made it easier for us to connect with more people. Knowing how to be introduced to the right people and fostering those relationships however, are skills that are frequently overlooked. How do some people meet the right people and others do not?

Meeting and connecting with people may be the greatest skill set you can develop. But how often do you sharpen this sword? When was the last time you asked yourself, "How efficient are my people meeting systems? Do I even give thought to the ways I meet people? Let me evaluate how effective I am in connecting with others."

Management expert, Peter Drucker is quoted in saying, "More business decisions occur over lunch and dinner than any other time, yet no MBA courses are given on the subject."

Where did you get your people meeting and connection training from? There are only far and few real world classes in the normal college curriculum. Where do brilliant entrepreneurs that have an amazing product know where to begin? What about the worker that has been in one industry for a while and wants to try to find a new career path, where do they start? How about college students that want to get a jump start on their career?

Most of the next three chapters will share tested methods that financial professionals use to build their clientele. The same methods can apply whether your connection expansion and relationship building is necessary for starting a business, career networking, or for a certain project that is important to you.

-Chapter Seven-

Expanding Connections

We are all familiar with the cliché, "It's not what you know, it's who you know." Today's social media age has made access to people easier than ever before. But there is more to networking than sending electronic friend requests and invitational emails. The easier networking is becoming by virtual standards, the more you need a purpose driven plan to meet the people you want to. Your contacts are your currency.

Meeting the people you want or need to meet comes down to two things: belief and process. If you believe in yourself, your project, your career, or your ability to help other people, then you should have no core issues in the pursuit of meeting the people you need to. If there is a lack of belief in any of those, then it will serve as mental trash that will get in the way of your people-meeting mission. After the belief is there, having a thought-out process of how to connect is necessary. This chapter will give you some ideas used by many financial professionals to build a business from scratch.

Before we go into different techniques to meet the people you need to in order to accelerate your professional development, it is important to remember the golden rule of networking. It is a two-way street. You need to get good at giving introductions to people to help them out first, before you can expect anything in return. And even if you give introductions, don't always expect something in return.

This chapter will explore techniques to develop a more purposeful network of contacts by leveraging today's technology with time-tested tactics no matter if you on are a career search, starting a new business or working on a project.

Start With What You Have

When financial advisors attend initial training, we ask them to write down 200 names of people they know. We call this the Project 200. The Project 200 is intended to help an advisor list each contact, their occupation, and how he or she is connected. This task is easy for career-changing advisors who have professional contacts throughout their years, but more difficult for a new advisor right out of college. Unless you just physically relocated or still take a yellow bus to school, you should have a Project 200. These people in your current circle will be valuable to help you meet your objectives.

If you are opening a new pizza restaurant, the first people you would tell are the closest people in your social circle. Your family and friends will probably share the word about your restaurant. It doesn't mean that you will coerce them into your shop and shove breadsticks down their throats. If you are on a new career search, starting a new business, or have a certain project you are passionate about, inform your close contacts. Ask them for help but don't oblige them. We often think to ourselves that asking for help is a sign of weakness but others often view it as a desire for advancement.

Even if you don't have a specific project or own a business, reflecting on your existing relationships often goes overlooked. Developing a "reconnection" plan with no professional intent is a great exercise to conduct. Losing contact with people is usually a mutual happening. You might feel guilty that you haven't talked to someone in a few years, but ask yourself, "have they been trying to contact me?" Life just gets busy and your old contacts would probably appreciate your reconnection plan. Maybe your plan states that every week you have at least two conversations, emails or coffee meetings with old contacts that you haven't talked to in over five years. You never know what you can learn about their professional paths and if you do decide to make a change in the future, the connection would have already been rejuvenated.

If you need to reach out to people that you lost contact with for direct business purposes, be up front. When you contact them to reconnect, let them know that it is for professional purposes but it would also give you a chance to catch up. Maybe one of the reasons you are changing your career path is to allow you the opportunity to spend more time building and rebuilding relationships with people versus spending all the hours in your day in front of a computer.

If you are looking to boost your sales this year, looking for a new career path, or looking to start your own business, start looking under your nose...or check book. Who do you currently support? Go through your credit card and checking account statements to see who you are giving business to. Whether it is your mechanic, hair stylist, or therapist, you are helping their business so they should have the courtesy of learning how they can help you or introduce you to others. Read your community newspapers and alumni magazines to see who may also be interested in meeting you. Participating in town board meetings, volunteering at a charity that you deeply care about and finding new hobbies are the basics of meeting new people.

Surveys: Reconnect, Research, Referred

Some financial services firms require a candidate to complete market surveys in the interviewing process. These surveys ask the candidate to speak with people about their perceptions and experiences with financial professionals. The first seven surveys are conducted with people that the candidate knows well. Then, the candidate tests their *referrability* by asking these contacts to introduce them to others in effort to meet new people in the area and ask them the same questions. The final eight surveys are completed with people the candidate has met from these introductions.

These surveys are exercises that test the candidate's comfort level with talking to people, asking for referrals, and understanding the perceptions of the marketplace. If you are looking to start your own business or switch industries, create a list of 10 relevant questions about your new venture or interests. These surveys can serve as your additional market research. Then call up people you know and schedule a meeting to talk about your thoughts and ambitions. If you get a meeting, take them through your customized market survey. Some questions might be:

"What are your thoughts and experiences about this industry or project?

"What would you like to see done differently in this industry?"

"Which areas of the business do you think I will excel in? Struggle with?"

"Who should I introduce myself to that can also provide some perspective?"

These advocates may help you along your way or bring some valuable insight to a problem you haven't considered. If you do decide to change paths, these contacts can refer you to other people who may help. They may become a Center of Influence for you.

Centers of Influence

A center of influence (COI) is a person you know or wish to know, who is well connected in a certain geographic or professional marketplace. This person has many contacts and is well respected in his or her network.

In most cases the COI is a professional who has influence in a certain network of people. Examples of COIs in the financial services industry are certified public accountants, attorneys, mortgage brokers, property and casualty insurance agents, and bankers. These professions have the power to refer their client to advisors. Think about your own career path. What other professions have close contacts with your industry? How can you leverage these contacts?

The second type of COI has a more general scope. These people are not directly involved in your industry, but they are well-respected professionals who are connected to many different types of people from all walks of life. Some examples may be a beloved professor at your college, the Executive Director of a non-profit organization, or the owners of a long-standing staple restaurant in town. Who are the COIs in your community that you should be fostering relationships with?

When you meet with your COIs and ask them about their own career paths. Learn about how they progressed in their careers. See if they are willing to introduce you to people who can help you. Some questions to ask are:

1. "How did you get to where you are today?"
2. "What advice do you have for me as I pursue this path?"
3. "Who are five people I should be meeting?"

These questions allow time for general business advice, personal advice, and introductions. Make sure to revisit this information and keep your COIs updated as you grow. If you try something one of your COI suggests, let them know your experience. Your COIs serve as your personal board of advisors to dispense advice and new connections as you move upward.

Spiderman

A great exercise is to look at your existing contacts and start webbing out the people that your contacts are naturally connected to. For example, say you are looking to get involved with an advertising firm and you have a meeting with your uncle who owns a restaurant in town. How can you make the most of that meeting assuming your uncle doesn't need any campaigns done for his bar and grill? Spider his likely contacts as a restaurant owner and look to be introduced to his network. This could be spouses of his wait staff, the chefs, his loyal customers, his landlord, neighboring businesses, his attorney, the food distributors, the liquor distributors, and the cleaning companies that come in to his business. Now think, who do those aforementioned people and professionals *know*?

You can even work this web backwards. If you know you want to meet a CEO at a certain company, spider his network back to the likely contacts that you have. Social media has made this so much easier to do. Take the CEO of the company. The CEO probably talks to other C level executives, spends their leisure time in the community and also has a good relationship with his assistant. You find out that his assistant is married to the athletic director at a local college.   A former colleague of yours, that you are close to, was the star football player at that college who can then start the introduction domino effect. Just be prepared, do some research and connect the dots.   It's a puzzle that you will spend time working on if your belief and passion for the purpose is in check.

Feeder Lists

Feeder lists help you get introduced to the people you want to meet. A friend of mine in the film industry asked me to help him with some career development ideas. He wanted to network with his existing contacts to see if they could introduce him to new contacts that might help him to advance the production of his feature film. His hope was that some new people could read his script or introduce him to a top notch agent.   I told him that every time he meets with someone to network with, he should prepare a feeder list.

A feeder list is simply a researched list of names that your own contact may be able to introduce you to. My friend would have to research whoever he was meeting with and see who they are likely to know, that he would like to meet. Preparing these feeder lists made him more prepared and the meeting more purposeful. When he would share the list and ask for introductions, the majority of the time his contacts would say "yes" and make the introduction.   Making feeder lists for every business and networking meeting can be one tool that greatly expands your contacts and gets you in front of the people you want to meet.

In order to prepare a successful feeder list, take a few minutes to research the person you are meeting with. The easiest way is to scan their contact lists on social media sites. If your contact is not on LinkedIn, do a Google search to determine their professional contacts.

After you schedule the meeting, make sure to be

clear that this meeting is for networking so you don't blindside the person.   When you meet, use language such as:

"John, I am glad we had the opportunity to meet.   As I said on the phone, I am looking to (change careers, build my business, meet people, etc.,) in the _____ field. I know you have had success building your career in _____.   The reason why I am (exploring, starting in, etc.) this field is because _____. With your permission, I'd like to brainstorm the names of people that I should be meeting. In preparation for our meeting I created a list of some professionals that you may or may not know. For example, I see that you are connected to Jane Smith on LinkedIn.   Could you tell me more about her? Would you have any objection to introducing me to her?   What would be the most comfortable way for you to make the introduction?"

Getting the introduction is half the battle but proper promotion and follow up is just as important.   Be sure to discuss the most efficient way for your nominator to follow through with making the introduction.

Another type of feeder list is a future (or dream) associates list.   In addition to creating individual lists for everyone you meet based on who you think they know, you share a list of ten people that could have the biggest impact on your career.   These names should sound familiar to most people that you are meeting with.

For example, if you owned a football helmets and pads business, meeting NFL owners or the commissioner would be very impactful.   You would then have a future associates list of Roger Goodell- Commissioner of the NFL, Bob Kraft- Owner New England Patriots, Jerry Jones- Owner of the Dallas Cowboys, etc.   You would share this with everyone you meet to see if they have any type of connections to these people.   They might not have direct connections with the people on the list, but they may be able to get you a degree closer. This also shows that you are thinking big about your career. People are attracted to those who think big and they are more likely to keep an eye out for you, versus the person looking to meet the athletic director at the local middle school.

Networking is a two way street. Ask the person if there are any contacts or people you can help him or her meet. Maybe their spouse is underemployed and looking for a new career, or maybe their son's soccer team needs a new sponsor and you know some local businesses that might be able to help. It may even be best to carry around a copy of your LinkedIn contacts in hard copy for people to thumb through.

Ideal Introductions

The more specific you are during these meetings, the better results you will have. Simply asking "Who should I be talking to?" or "Who could give me advice?" makes your contact person think too much and the meeting will not be productive. Remember, getting introduced to others is your responsibility. You need to take the work out of it for the introducer (also known as the nominator). The best way is through the Ideal Introduction.

There was a commercial for Autotrader.com that featured a man who screamed, "I want a new car." Thousands of cars appeared. The man proceeded to tell us the traits of his preferred car. If he said, "I want a two door," only two door cars appeared. He followed it with, "I want a sports car, a red one." The choices narrowed. Finally, he said "a convertible." He was rewarded with the car he wanted, all because he was able to articulate exactly what he wanted. If you want people to help you, you need to tell them how. The Ideal Introduction is a thought-out description of the type of person you are looking to meet. You should be able to convey exactly who you are looking to build relationships with. If you can't articulate who you are looking to be introduced to, how can you expect others to help?

For example, financial advisors in a networking meeting might ask, "Do you know any forward-thinking and responsible business owners in the Bay area, who have been in business for at least five years and have five or more employees?" Describing personal values can help make a deeper connection. A business owner can have five employees in Oakland and make seven figures a year, but if he isn't forward thinking and responsible, he might not be a good fit for financial planning. What are the qualities, values or descriptive features of the people that you would want to meet?

Transferrable Skills to the Dating Scene

If you are single and searching for a compatible partner, you can adapt some of these techniques. Few people put together a mindful introduction plan for love, but it might just give you the best results.

If you followed this plan, the first thing to do is to meet with some of your best friends. Think of the friends that are particularly outgoing or have careers that allow them to constantly meet people. These friends can serve as your dating centers of influence.

Your next step is to meet with these friends, share your interests, and show that you are being proactive. Ask about friends you know they have. You might even want to go to their social media pages and look at their friends that may be single. If there appears to be a good match, ask for an introduction.

Some friends will try to introduce you to every single person they know. This is probably not going to be helpful. Be specific about what you are looking for in a date. For example, you might say:

"I am looking for a guy between the ages of 26

and 30 who lives in the Boston area with a steady career and doesn't work nights. I prefer a college graduate who has family in the Northeast. It would also help if he has a great sense of humor and isn't too rigid or uptight. I would prefer them to be slightly more extroverted than introverted and taller than me. It would be a bonus if they enjoy going to Celtics games and spending time outdoors. Does anyone come to mind?"

Being specific about your needs will be far more helpful than asking, "Do you know any single guys around here?"

As much as I may be writing in jest, there is much to be said about dating purposefully rather than by default. By applying these people meeting techniques, it could save everyone time, and create more longstanding relationships.

Networking Events

Extroverted business owners love receiving an invitation to a networking event. While there may be many prospective clients at these events, there will also be competitors. You need to network smartly and with intent.

Before the event, conduct research on the networking group to see who may attend. Ask the coordinator of the event who usually shows up. Make a plan. Set a goal to have three meaningful conversations with people you don't know.

The point of networking is to meet new people. It is good to go with someone you know, but make sure to branch out. Perhaps the person you're with can introduce you to other people that he or she knows, and vice versa. This can be an easy way to break the ice with new people, and you both benefit from the deal.

Networking events shouldn't be the place for sales pitches or cheerleading sessions for your company. Don't talk too much about your business or ambitions. Instead, connect on a personal level with people. If you make a good connection, follow up with a meeting or phone call after the event. At the very least, try to track them down on LinkedIn. Networking is worthless unless you follow up with the people. Connect with a new contact within 48 hours. I'll never forget the day I saw a veteran advisor mentoring a new professional. The newbie had a stack of 14 business cards sitting on his desk that he accrued at a networking event a week ago. The veteran took the cards, ripped them up, and threw them in the trash, saying:

"If you didn't call already, you never had a reason to and you never will."

-Chapter Eight-

Professionalism and the Third-First Impression

I vividly remember sitting at Starbucks in between classes while attending college in New York City. A gentleman in his 70s, who appeared to be homeless, sat down next to me and simply said, "The more things change, the more they should stay the same." I never quite understood why that person and his comment entered my life. But the more advanced we get in communicating with people through technology, the more we need to stay grounded in basic professionalism and relationship-building skills.

Nowadays, when you meet with someone for the first time, there are typically two impressions that were previously made about you. The first impression might be your Internet presence. What comes up when someone Google's your name? Or what images do your social media profiles project? If your first impression isn't coming from the web then the person you are meeting may perceive you in the same light that they perceive the nominator (the person who introduced the two of you).

The second "first" impression is the way you contacted the person you want to meet. What medium did you choose? How was your email structured? How did you sound on the phone? The third -first impression is when you meet face to face. This chapter will discuss making good impressions and building relationships that you currently have.

The Phone and Text

If you look at your DAD System, you may have had a lot of new connection points that never materialized into relationship builder points. The only way to turn those connections into meaningful contacts is to meet with that person face-to-face or have a detailed phone conversation. The old school way of setting up appointments is by making a phone call. Generation Y hesitates to call a restaurant to place a takeout order nowadays since they can order on the web, never mind the hesitation they have in making a professional contact.

Gen Y grew up during the "telemarketing boom" in the 80s, 90s and early 2000s. They were trained by their parents not to pick up the phone during dinnertime because it would be a sales call. Some parents even used their children to screen their calls! Then a clever invention called Caller ID was a family dinner godsend, followed by the "Do Not Call" list. If you are reading this book you probably aren't really looking for a career as a telemarketer, however the psychological impact associated with making phone calls for initial contact in a professional way has been damaging.

The first rule of phoning when trying to connect with someone for the first time is to never sell or cheerlead on the phone. Make the phone call about an introduction, not a sales pitch. The goal of the initial phone call is to set up a time when two professionals can meet each other (or have a future, in depth call to learn more about each other).

Whether it is for career purposes, sales purposes, or help with a project, make the meeting about two professionals getting together to see if you can be a resource for each other. From there you can see if there are any mutual benefits.

If there is a nominator, or someone who introduced you to the person on the other end, mention this early in the call. This will bring a level of personal connection that distinguishes you from the thousands of telemarketers that may be calling this person.

"Hi Joe? Joe, this is Jack, I am a friend of your colleague Jill, did I catch you at a bad time? Did Jill give you a heads up that I would be reaching out?

If you don't have a nominator, mention that you connected with him or her on a social media site to bring familiarity. If you don't even have a social media connection on your side, then the call is considered cold. You need to dig for some type of commonality between you and the person to better your chances of a successful call.

If you are granted a face-to-face meeting with the person, make sure you state your expectations of your time together on the phone call. You may be calling to network, to share ideas of how you can do business with each other, or to ask for feedback on something you are working on. The clearer your expectations, the more productive the meeting will be. If the person is hesitant to meet with you but you persist and gain the appointment, make note of it. This will need to be remembered when you do meet with the person.

Make sure to monitor your tone to project confidence and casualness. If you don't, the other person will keep their defensive guard up. Albert Mehrabian, Professor Emeritus at UCLA, is noted for conducting a very common yet misinterpreted study around communication. He notes that communication is made up of 55 percent body language, 38 percent tone and 7 percent words when sending messages. During the phone call, the person on the other end cannot see your body language, so tone becomes 93 percent of the message.

In training, we often have financial professionals record their phone calls into a tape recorder. They dread hearing themselves during the playback, but it is an effective learning tool. Normally their tone and pace with a potential client sounds very different than it would when they talk to a friend or family member. Record yourself on a few professional or introduction calls. You may cringe listening to yourself, but it is a valuable learning device.

The jury is still out on *professional* text messaging but it is becoming a more and more acceptable means of communication. The two circumstances where it is not acceptable are in managing conflict with another person or in making initial contact with someone you do not know. When most Gen Yers get a phone call from a number they do not recognize, they often do to not pick up and would have preferred a text message to see the purpose of the call. Gen Y to Gen Y initial contact is almost acceptable through text, with the caveat of the 10 cent cost. Gen Y to other generations is a risk. If the text message is professional and sets the expectation of a phone call to follow, then it may go appreciated but email is probably the safer way to go. It's less intimate and invasive than a text but unfortunately could just get mixed in with other junk email. Text messaging should not be a substitute for a phone call for people in sales based careers but it can certainly be an accompaniment or contingency method.

The Myth of Destiny Changers

Getting introduced to influential people is a great feeling. Imagine the screenwriter who gets a chance to pitch his script to Martin Scorsese or Tim Burton, or the female pop singer who has the chance to sing for Simon Cowell or Madonna. These are rare, nerve-racking experiences. Our EGA will blast. We view these meetings as destiny changers.

There is no such thing as a destiny-changing meeting. Another person cannot change your destiny. Yes, you need to meet the right people and highly influential people can make things happen. However, putting all of our weight into an introduction or a meeting reduces our chances of getting the results we want.

Happiness and success are achieved by the proper management of expectations. When people get important meetings, they often believe they will walk out of the meeting a completely changed person. That rarely happens, especially when you meet with someone who didn't solicit you for the introduction. More than likely, you'll receive "This makes sense and I like the idea, but it's not the right time" or "lets connect again in a few months, glad we met." Just because you didn't have the fantasy scenario doesn't mean that the meeting went poorly.

When you get an important meeting, don't overexcite yourself or discredit yourself. Relax and act like you belong there, because you do— you secured the meeting. Many professionals, no matter the type of business they are in, get in front of an influential person and become star struck. They speed up their pace, mess up their body language and project insecurity. No one wants to do business with that type of person. Be appreciative, but not gushing. Thank them for their time, but don't put them on a pedestal. Don't relinquish your personal power. Remember, you got the meeting. You belong there. You could bring value to this person's career. The more successful they are, the more confident you need to be, internally. No one can take complete credit for changing your destiny. Only you.

Professionalism 101

Some may call this subchapter "common sense 101," but you would be amazed at how many experienced professionals—meaning in the workforce for ten plus years—do not have the professional basics down. And to their defense, unless they took some courses or had a caring mentor along the way, some of this content may have slipped through the career development cracks. Nothing can kill rapport or bulldoze a new relationship more than disobeying a few professionalism basics. I know you know this already, but let's just cover our bases.

Rule number one in professionalism, is to redefine "on time" as "five minutes early." Punctuality is more important than you think. If a prospective advisor candidate is more than three minutes late without a phone call or heads up, some recruiters deny them an interview. Nothing shows a lack of personal responsibility more than being late (unless you live in Miami). Of course, there are always uncontrollable circumstances. Traffic shouldn't be one, unless it was your car that caused the traffic jam. If the interstate is shut down for five hours because of a gasoline rollover and it's on the news, you may be off the hook. But a normal traffic jam, no excuse. Nothing bothers me more than when someone walks in late to an important meeting with a Dunkin' Donuts cup. You were running late, but you put your caffeine addiction ahead of the organization? If you want to bring coffee in, that's fine, but be on time.

A firm (but not dominating) handshake and eye contact are Chapter One in the introduction bible. I am amazed at the number of dead-fish handshakes and the lack of eye contact I see in the marketplace. Nothing showcases a lack of confidence more than a weak handshake. You can also read a personality by the angle of the handshake. If the person you are meeting comes in over the top, with his or her palms almost facing completely to the ground, they may have a more dominant personality and want you to subconsciously know that from the start of the conversation. If they have more of a palm up handshake, then they usually are more reserved, shy and don't need to feel like they are in control. A mutual handshake comes up from the side, palms to the side. If you want to be more welcoming and inviting to the person, slightly tilt the palms upward. After the initial handshake, step off to the side of the person you are speaking with. If you stand directly in front of them, it signals to their brain that they cannot flee the situation…you are blocking their "flight," so subconscious thoughts of "fight" might come over them. Not the best feelings to start off a relationship with.

When you introduce yourself, you should use your first and last name, because you are building a reputation for yourself. If you are waiting for someone to arrive, maybe in a lobby, be aware of your body language. Be standing up, not slouched on a chair. Your physiology plays on your inner confidence, not just on how you are perceived by someone else.

When you are meeting someone and it is evident that their day is upside down on them, recognize it. Ask them if they would like to reschedule for a time that may be better for them. This may be disheartening for you, but their full attention is not going to be on you anyway. The person will more than likely appreciate the consideration and respect you for not having a self-centered agenda.

Dress Basics

With more industries moving to business casual or simply casual, it is important to be aware of the more traditional, business attire. Here are some basics for the gentlemen out there. Shoe color matches your belt color.

The tip of your tie should fall down to your belt buckle. Wear a belt! Make sure you take the tag on the sleeve of the suit off. It is comical to see how many new graduates leave that tag on. Don't button the bottom button on your blazer.   Don't wear athletic socks with your dress shoes- wear dress socks. Clean or shine your shoes.   Wear a white t-shirt under your dress shirt. If you need to be colorful, do so with your tie versus your shirt. Studies show that it's more professional and people will trust you more if you wear a white-based or business blue shirt. Don't wear striped ties with striped shirts; you will look like an optical illusion.   Don't wear button down collared shirts when you wear a suit. It's okay with a blazer. When in doubt, shave.   Save the light colored suits for the summer and more laid back meetings. Take off your hemp bracelets.   Don't dangle your key chain out of your pocket. Hide tattoos.

I defaulted to a female colleague of mine to suggest the best dress practices for females. Wear clothing that fits you. Avoid tight clothes that ride up when sitting or walking.   Choose business staples first; a couple of dark suits, a tan or black length-appropriate skirt, and a couple of crisp button down shirts. When purchasing a suit, twist the fabric of the sleeves and hold it in place for 10 seconds, if it wrinkles then think twice about the purchase. You can add colored or print pieces to a neutral wardrobe and have multiple outfits to choose from.   Dresses can also be appropriate as long as they are tailored with full coverage. Dresses should fall to just above the knee or to knee length.

Beware of Professional Visiting

Now that you are on time and look good, let's talk about the meeting. When new advisors come into the business they try to book up their calendar with appointments. Unfortunately, many of these appointments become professional visits. Professional visiting isn't a positive term in financial services. It basically means burning time. Don't just meet for meetings sake. Many new advisors will look at their calendar and see that it is full of appointments. That is a good thing. However, if you don't get down to business and have meaningful discussions with the people you are meeting with, you are just visiting them. No matter what your profession is, if you don't show some type of value or how you can possibly work with people in the future, it can be a waste of time.

When I was working on a few creative projects earlier in my career, I had no problem reaching out to a very successful person to set up a meeting. The mistake that I would frequently make is that I would meet some great people that could help in their creative endeavor, but I didn't get down to business. I wanted them to like me first and then when my timing was perfect, I would go back to them when I was ready for their help or partnership. That feeling of "perfect timing" would never come. Perfection is the enemy of progress.

When you meet with someone, set an expectation for the meeting and make sure the person knows the general premise of the meeting. You should also set your own expectation of what you are looking to achieve by having this meeting.

The next step is to create an agenda. Send it out beforehand so that everyone can come prepared. It speeds up every process. By giving meeting invitees a heads up, they have a chance to do their own research on the topic at hand. That leads to a more meaningful conversation and a better use of everyone's time.

Always have a pen and paper when meeting with someone. Ipads are becoming more acceptable. Don't take feverish notes on everything he or she says. This is distracting. Keep eye contact. If you need to take notes, jot down a word or phrase here and there so you remember the context.   Have a decent pen and have it readily available so you aren't searching for it. It's always good to have a back-up pen as well.

Respect someone's time. If they had time for a 20-minute meeting, at 18 minutes ask if he or she has time to continue or if you should schedule another time to reconnect. When someone is in their office in front of the computer, they are probably working. Be polite and respectful of this. If you need to interrupt, keep your communication brief, and ask if there is a better time to meet.

Leave five minutes at the end to capture the meeting. Summarize the meeting, review assignments, and create a plan to follow-up. This capturing process will keep momentum, outline clear expectations for each other, and tie the meeting together. Think of meetings as if you are blowing air into a balloon, and this capturing process as you tying the knot at the end to keep all the air in. Send out a follow-up letter to participants restating everything you captured in the meeting. This documents the priorities and keeps the momentum going.   Also, if you misinterpreted anything from the meeting, it gives the person a chance to correct you.   Lastly, if you deem it appropriate, test out your ideal introduction language to meet other people that you could help or that you enjoy meeting with.

Making the Most of the Meeting

Earlier in the chapter we noted Mehrabian's communication study that states communication is made up of 55 percent body language, 38 percent tone and 7 percent words when sending messages. This occurs mostly in messages of emotion. The three parts of the message must be congruent in order to be effective. If there is an ambiguous conversation or there is incongruence between those three parts of the message, then the receiver would tend to favor the non-verbal elements for the true message. That said, responding to the body language of the person you are conversing with can solidify your message. Most often you want to mirror and match the movements of the other person, with subtle transitions. Unless the person is anxious or uneasy, then you want to adjust your body language and tone to be more inviting and comforting. Ask them questions to understand their nervousness.

You can read books on body language that will list all different movements and what those motions are saying about the person's feelings. But memorizing all the possible movements can be a challenge. Many times body language can be figured out in a logical manner. For example, if someone is hesitant to say something, they will often put their hand over their mouth or curl and press their lips together. Almost as if they are trying to physically prevent themselves from speaking. If they are frustrated, they will often rub the back of their neck, as if they are massaging the stress away. If someone is tugging on their ear, you are probably talking their ear *off* because that is often a sign they want to interrupt you. Being a fanatical observer of body language will make you a master of communication.

An off statement can sabotage your image. People we know well might overlook an off-statement, but new connections will be judging everything we say or do. I did a large intern training one summer. After I introduced a guest speaker and went to my office to work on my computer, one of the interns walked in and asked if he could leave a little bit early that day. So I asked him why. He responded, "I am a bit tired and just want to go home." Are you kidding me? At least say you feel really sick!

Another time, I was part of a networking group with a bunch of professionals, when a middle-aged disheveled man staggered in. He stood up and said, "You know what they say, if you show up on time and not hung over, you are beating most people." Everyone laughed. I'm not sure who created that quote, but it isn't a standard you should be living by for growth. Needless to say, he wasn't referred much business after that day.

Developing a Follow Up Plan

When advisors have a substantial client base, they need to learn to be selective with their time. They learn to treat all of their clients fairly, but not equally. The A+ and A clients are the clients who care about their plans, who have the most money invested, give the most referrals and should continue to give business in the future. Advisors will typically give the A+ clients the most "touch-points" throughout the year— birthday cards, holiday cards, newsletters, charity event invitations, reasonable small gifts, etc. On the other hand, assistants or associate advisors are hired to make sure that the C and D clients are being serviced properly.

Ask any golfer you know about how the people they play with will influence their level of play. If the golfer's average score is 85 and he plays with a bunch of hackers who can't break 100, you will see that golfer typically score higher than 85. But if they played with a bunch of scratch golfers shooting in the low 70s, you will see that golfer shoot way below his average of 85. You subconsciously adjust your level of play to who you are playing with. The same holds true in the professional world. Your income is the average of your five closest friends. Your behaviors will mirror those of whom you surround yourself with. So who do you spend the most time with? Your DAD System can help you reflect on this. Set your meals and relationship builders to include more people that you aspire to be like.

Segment your own professional and personal contacts and develop a communication plan for your groupings.

Are you spending adequate time with the people who best serve your life and goals? Who gets a birthday phone call, email, or card? Who is on the quarterly dinner regiment? Who gets a round of golf in the summer? Who gets the quarterly lunch or after work cocktail? Whether friends, business contacts or newer relationships, make a plan for building and fortifying the relationships that are important to you.

-Chapter Nine-

Human Connectivity

When Gen Y hears the word connectivity, their mind often jumps to how strong of a WiFi or phone signal they have. The stronger the connectivity signal the easier and faster they can have access to information and the more productive they can be. In this chapter we will be talking about devices to boost your *human* connectivity.

Having a compelling vision, ample knowledge and an abundance of contacts is a recipe for a successful career. But a skill set that can be a magnet for your highest level of success is the art of understanding someone and applying the appropriate path in connecting with them.

Human understanding is more important than ever before because everyone has access to the same information now. Relating to people trumps "wowing" people with your vast array of knowledge. If people had the time and wanted to conduct their due diligence, they may be able to find much of the information you are about to share with them, on their own...even from their smart phone. You can search for true markups on cars while you are negotiating with the dealer. You can look up asset allocation models and retirement calculators while you are sitting across the table from a financial advisor. You can write your will faster on LegalZoom then it would take you to commute to your attorney's office. I am not trying to diminish the value of expertise, but rather show how important it is to understand the people you are communicating with. You need to be able to connect with people more than a search bar, drop down menu or check boxes on a website can.

The first task at hand in human connectivity is to reduce nervousness in a new or business relationship. In order to ease tension and build a deeper connection from the beginning of a conversation with a new connection, use your small talk to show commonality. If you were referred to the person by another colleague or if the two of you have a mutual friend, it would be best to use your warm up talk on the relationship bonds you have in common. A human connection is most potent. Find out how long they have known the other person or what activities or organizations they are a part of with the nominator. People feel comfortable if their villages are connected.

Many times you will meet with someone without having any contacts in common. You could probably do some Internet research on the person now to learn more about them. Don't talk religion or politics with someone when you are developing a new relationship. Even be careful of your biases in terms of current events that are going on. If there is a particular hobby you share in common, first recognize that you also have an interest in the hobby but then make the dialogue about the other person's interest in the topic. Be interested, not interesting.

For example, if you both like golf, share that you love golf but then don't make the rest of the conversation about your country club, set of clubs, or what you shot the other day. Ask those questions of the other person. People will feel good about themselves and you, if they do the majority of the talking. Certainly answer if they inquire about you.

Professionalism Doesn't Secure Human Connectivity

Some statements you will never forget. I was working with a former Marine who was transitioning back into the work force. He had spent years in Iraq but didn't speak too much about his former career. He was smart, had a great work ethic and had a gentle personality. He was off to a slower than expected start a few months into building his financial services practice and he decided to reach out to me for some ideas, motivation, and venting. He went on and spewed out a number of different reasons why he wasn't excelling. Then I asked him to sum it up with one issue. He said, "It was easier to have bullets shot at me by people in a foreign war, than connecting with people through a professional conversation in my own backyard."

We dug a little bit deeper into what was happening with his prospective clients when he was meeting with them. His problem boiled down to a human connectivity issue. We later discovered he was more concerned about coming across as professional and having all the answers than he was concerned with understanding the person he was meeting with. More specifically, he struggled with understanding someone's decision zones. This is a level of human connectivity where you can diagnose and prescribe the correct amount of information, feelings, and energy that a situation warrants and can move someone to make a decision in a comfortable and natural way. I had to give him a framework to follow in his interactions. I didn't want him to feel like he was at war when he was simply talking to people in a professional environment.

I designed a decision zone tool for him that paid homage to his former career to help him help people make buying or business decisions.   I thought the best way to help him was to simplify people into a few different decision making zones. I am aware that human beings are all different. I am aware that we all come from different backgrounds, have different values, beliefs, aptitudes, weaknesses, and personality traits. But to help in human connectivity and around helping people make decisions, we need to start with a few types of hardwiring that people may have. I decided to break down the three mindsets or zones, when it comes to making decisions. People make professional, business, or buying decisions either in the AIR, on LAND or in the SEA.

Decision Zones

	HINT	APPROACH	DRIVER
AIR	Altruistic	Inclusive	Relationship
LAND	Logical	Analytical	Numbers & Details
SEA	Self	Ego/Energy	Achievement

Coding

There is a coding for each decision zone in this device. The first letter in each zone is the "hinting" word. This will help you pick up on clues as to what decision zone the person you are interacting with will likely fall in. During your interactions do they tip off being altruistic, logical or more self-centric? Self-centric doesn't necessarily mean selfish. It means that they take extra pride in their self-image. You can find these hints through asking open-ended questions and by just making observations. You may want to cater your warm-up conversation or small talk to be more intentional in extracting clues. The first letter again will help you with clues on what zone the person might fall in.

After you understand the probable decision zone of the people you are interacting with, remember how to connect with them to aid them in a decision-making process. The second letter in the zone coding signifies the tactical approach that would best work to help move the person into a decision making process. Should you be using a very inclusive approach that is highly sensitive to the other person's feelings? Should you use a heavy dosage of analytical metrics and data to help the person make a decision? Or should you use energy and show the person how the decision appeals to their ego?

The third letter (and forth for LAND) in the zone codes represents the key driver or end results that the decision maker cares the most about or is most motivated by. Even though you may have used a certain approach to sell to the person or interact at a deeper level, knowing how to follow up and stay connected with the person is most important. Again, it doesn't matter if the person is your client, your employee, your employer, or your business partner.

Use these statements as a general guideline:

When in the AIR, make sure you fly the friendly skies.

When on LAND, stay grounded in the facts.

When in the SEA, use waves of energy.

Understanding Your Zone

Before you can start picking up on people's decision zones, it's best to first understand what zone you likely operate in. Once you achieve this, you can then properly acclimatize your approach to help connect more effectively with others. Reflect on how you have made big decisions in your life, some recent decisions or just your general motivators. You may feel as though you could fall into all three decision zones, which is normal, however you are probably hard-wired to default to one in particular. Ask yourself some of the questions below or even go back to your parents or people who knew you when you were young to get their opinion of how your mind was designed.

A couple questions might help:

What statement best describes you during a group project?

I want to be a great teammate and have people appreciate working with me.   (AIR)

I care about why we are doing this project, how it works, and I work with the details to ensure we have a well thought out and near perfect solution. (LAND)

I want to control the group and motivate people to win even if it means not having all the information or everyone love me. (SEA)

I care most about having:

A high concern for cooperation.   (AIR)

Attention to detail and appreciation of data. (LAND)

High energy and the big picture. (SEA)

I describe power as:

Solid and plentiful relationships. (AIR)

Knowledge and correct choices. (LAND)

Achievements, successful image, and money. (SEA)

I am most offended by the following statement:

I do not know many people that care about me or consider me their friend. (AIR)

I don't plan things out and I frequently make mistakes and wrong decisions. (LAND)

I am not seen as being very successful. (SEA)

Once you have established the zone that you usually make decisions in and what your mind defaults to, be mindful in how you interact with others. It is human nature to use that same methodology when interacting with other people in sales, business, or decision-making conversations. Knowing what you default to and being aware of how that either connects you or disconnects you from the other zones is critical.

You might be thinking that if you have the same mindset or decision zone as the person you are interacting with, then there will instantly be a connection. That is not necessarily true. In fact, it can actually slow down the decision-making process.

If you are an AIR zoner and you meet with another AIR zoner, then you may fall victim to too much personal talk and not enough engagement about the decision or professional topic at hand. You may become best friends by the end of your time together, but perhaps no decisions were made or no actions were taken.

If you and the person you are interacting with are both LAND zoners, then you may overdose on data. You both may get caught up in too many irrelevant details and never move to action because you both are concerned about finding the absolute perfect solution or decision. Chasing perfect often leads to inaction.

If you both are SEA zoners, then you may have egotistical issues and struggle with figuring out who the biggest fish in the sea is. You may butt heads and your dominating personalities might prevent decisions from being made.

The AIR Zoners

AIR Hints = Altruistic

A person will hint that he or she is an AIR zoner if their language and persona is others focused or altruistic. Listen to their dialogue. He or she may be an AIR zoner if they are asking questions about you personally and socially instead of sizing you up professionally. When they speak, they may be open to sharing their feelings with you. They tend to be more emotional in their dialogue than the other zoners.

AIR zoners will come also across more welcoming in their dialogue, often with more casual and "warm up" conversation then with other zoners. When they answer questions, they will revert to relationships or a team-focused response versus what they individually accomplished. Family, friends, and relationships that are important to them will pop up frequently in conversation. They will use the word "we" instead of "I". AIR zoners will usually be good conversationalists, meaning they'll exhibit a proper balance of back and forth dialogue. They will look to avoid conflict at most costs unless they are extremely emotionally charged and feel deeply offended.

Of the three zones, AIR zoners will be most willing to meet with you and spend time with you.   So if you reflect on your point of initial contact with someone and it was very easy to get a meeting with them or they didn't ask too much about the agenda or business at hand, it may be a tip off that they operate in the "AIR".   That being said, they may have met five other people just like you already this month. AIR zoners are easier to initially connect with, but may be harder to move to business action if your relationship building isn't sincere…even if you really do have a valuable proposition for them.

AIR zoners tend to dress more casual, not needing the immediate attention by way of appearance.   Their emails may be more personalized than the other zones and rarely ever cookie cutter.   They should be more open to connecting on social networks and introducing you to people they have relationships with.

AIR Approach= Inclusive

If the hints have shown the person you are interacting with is an AIR zoner, then the key approach to connect with them and help them make decisions is to be very inclusive. You need to make sure their feelings are always taken into account when making the decision. Don't try to rush them to a conclusion- you must hand hold and ask them how they are feeling at each step of the process. Invite their opinions, communicate in a relaxed tone and show a personal interest.   It may also help to show how this decision will benefit any other relationships they have with others.

Always give AIR zoners an opportunity to speak, and share with them how they make you feel or anything that you have learned from them. The more you can show them that you are also learning from them, the stronger the relationship bond will be. That is a key to the AIR zoner.

Take care of the detailed work for them but don't talk down to them. Make sure that with all your interactions, the conversation never begins, ends, or is only focused on the transaction or business task at hand.

Some easy language in building connectivity with AIR zoners is stating or asking:

"I was thinking of you the other day because….."

"How does _____ make you feel?"

Never have a cookie cutter approach with an AIR zoner; try to be as customizable as possible. Show how the features, benefits, or whatever the decision that you are presenting can specifically help their lives and the people around them. Have a fun time with AIR zoners as well. They will care most about going to an event, to dinner, or to do some other activity that has nothing to do with the business relationship.

The best vehicle to move forward in the AIR zone is a JET.

Judge Everything Together

AIR Driver = Relationship

Always work on your personal relationship with an AIR zoner after a decision has been made. Stay connected to them through frequent check-ins and with specific questions exclusive to their situation. As long as the professional relationship is intact, concentrate heavily on building a blended, personal relationship. Remember the things that are important to them outside of the professional world, like their birthdates, dog's names, career milestones, etc. The handwritten note or random phone call is most appreciated by AIR zoners. AIR zoners respond best to those who pay attention to their feelings over a long period of time.

The LAND Zoners

LAND Hints= Logical

LAND zoners care about the facts. They aren't too concerned about the relationship but are more concerned with making the best possible decision based on the details and numbers. The clues that show you are dealing with a LAND zoner are that they will tend to ask the most questions, and the focus of the questions is data gathering, rather than personal or emotionally driven questions. They will do more asking than telling, but when they tell you something, it will be knowledge based, not feeling based. They will tell you what they know or have researched. They may revert to the past and to historical data or past decisions they have made and how those results panned out. Their words and actions will tend to be slow, reactionary and cautious.

LAND zoners are usually very organized, neat, and methodical. Listen for dialogue that includes order, coordination, process and prefacing. They are very concerned with the details and might correct themselves more often than it really matters, especially in reflecting on events or order. If the person you are interacting with actually reads your materials, literature, or presentations they are probably LAND zoners. Their emails may tend to be lengthy, prefaced with outlines, spell checked, have proper grammar, and contain more questions to gather necessary data.

LAND Approach = Analytical

Get your facts straight when you are dealing with LAND zoners. Being too friendly or personable might come across as superficial. Make sure you do a thorough job in explaining your concepts the first time around so you develop a stronger connection, and tune them in right away. Be comprehensive with detailed specifications and even historical data that are applicable to the situation. Always double-check your work. Careless mistakes will lead to immediate disconnection.

Be careful not to jump to conclusions with the LAND zoners and avoid being vague. They will be turned off and disconnect from you if you try to get them to act quickly, however LAND zoners are prone to dragging out their decision making process. To prevent them from elongating the process, be very specific in what the next steps are. Lay out the entire proposition, process, or product step-by-step for them, but make sure you have an end point. Create a checklist of mini decisions and a progression path for them. Speak in outline fashion. For example, use terms like "First we will evaluate this, second we will…" Avoid giving LAND zoners too many options or choices to select from. This will hinder them from action and decisiveness, as they'll try to break down the details of every option.

Some language to use with LAND zoners when trying to move them to action:

"What information do you need in order to make the most accurate decision?"

"We will not finalize the decision until you have all the details, but which numbers (or details) are you most concerned with right now? What are you least concerned with?

LAND zoners feel that knowledge is power and might not want to admit if they do not understand something. Instead of saying, "Does this make sense?" or "Is this clear?" put it back on you by asking, "Am I making sense in my explanation?" This is important because they probably won't make a decision unless they understand everything thoroughly. However, they might not want to admit to you that they aren't understanding a particular concept.

LAND zoners don't want to be wrong because of a lack of research or thought. Frequently check in on their thoughts around the decision. Ask them what they think is the best deal, solution, or path to take in the decision at hand. Then follow it up with what they think the biggest consequence will be if they make a mistake. When it comes to complex decisions, people often do nothing at all. Try to frame the decision in terms of the consequences of inaction versus action.

> The best vehicle to use when working in
> the LAND zone is a TANK.
>
> Think About Necessary Knowledge

LAND Driver= Numbers and Details

You can continue and deepen your connection with LAND zoners by feeding them factual data or new, proven processes on how to further enhance the decisions they have already made. If you absorb any knowledge that they would also enjoy, send it off to them. Also, make periodical presentations to them that show the results of any important decisions they have made with your help. Feel free to say, "Hey, you were right!"

Keep your opinions or spins to yourself and keep feeding data driven reports. Congratulate them on the correct choices they have made while offering improvement strategies on the choices that didn't pan out. Feel free to get their insight or detail-driven opinions on projects or strategies that are important to you to continue to strengthen the connection.

The SEA Zoners

SEA Hints= Self

SEA zoners tend to be more confident and image conscious than the other zones. In dialogue, they will usually be telling you about themselves or what they think. They tend to use the word "I" versus "we" or "my" versus "our". They will speak in more general terms and not get specific with details or irrelevant numbers. They will get to the point more quickly than the other two zones and their pace of dialogue can come across as rushed. As stated before, as much as we are using the word self as the hinting word, that doesn't mean they are selfish or that they don't care about others. They tend to naturally come across as dominant and take pride in their image. If they speak about their successes or about accomplishments in general, then they may be a SEA zoner. You may view a SEA zoner as controlling and competitive.

SEA zoners may assert their confidence through the way they dress, the car they drive, or other materialistic items.   They will be more label-conscious and are motivated by recognition. Sometimes you can get tripped when dealing with a very humble SEA zoner.   All the above can be very important to them but they don't ever "show and tell."   Instead, look for examples that support if the person has a very strategic mindset that is big picture focused.

SEA zone emails will be brief and to the point, and may be even neglect any spelling or grammar errors. Their LinkedIn profiles will typically be left unfinished but will to showcase their accomplishments. They favor the 30,000 foot view versus the details.

SEA Approach= Ego/Energy

As much as SEA zoners might dominate your conversation, you will probably always know where you stand with them.   To start off, always recognize their accomplishments and their results.   Raise your level of energy and ego to a certain level when you meet with these people. They typically want to affiliate themselves with other successful people so raise your image a few notches.

Be enthusiastic and confident. Be energized and let them know that you are really good at what you do, but make sure they understand that they are still in control and the ball will always be in their court.

Keep your message high-level and big picture. Don't bore SEA zoners with the details. Always connect these decisions to an accomplishment or a goal that they care about. Always be willing to cooperate with them but never sacrifice being straightforward and direct. How does this decision affect their bottom line or their image? Think big with SEA zoners and think futuristically. Don't complain or sweat the small stuff when around them.

> The best vehicle to use while working in the SEA zone is a SUB.
>
> Simple- Useful- Big picture

SEA Driver =Achievement

Deepening the relationship with a SEA zoner can be a challenge. It is always good to follow up and stay connected with them but be sure not to waste their time with irrelevant information or dialogue. Much like the approach to help them make a decision, appealing to their ego throughout the years can help deepen the connection as long as it doesn't come across as heavy schmoozing. Compliment them on their achievements, especially if you helped them in getting there. Following up with them can be powerful if you can bring ideas and action plans on how to get them to achieve more or progress further towards a goal, of course with them taking control.

Always recognize their successes and show ways that can help them achieve something else that is important to them.

Connection Camouflage Conclusions

Many times you will work very hard to network and find people that could help you in your professional development or career. Unfortunately, most people will "wing it" once they have meetings set up with people. Even if the purpose of the meeting is to learn more about another professional for future networking purposes, you should have a plan or connection strategy in place.

The decision zones can act as your connection camouflage when meeting with people. It is one more tool to help stack the deck in your favor for developing a relationship. Even if there isn't an apparent decision on the table, there will always be the decision of whether or not that person will want to work for or with you, introduce people to you, or make time for you in the future. If we can identify how someone is likely to make decisions, what approach or way to interact with them, and what they care most about, it will better the chances of a strong connection.

-Concluding Summary-

Using the DAD System heightens the focus on your daily activities of learning and people to accelerate you to your long-term goals. If you permit, other people may help you grow through accountability and feedback. The game also grants you the opportunity to help other people grow where they want to grow.

Self-Coaching

After you define what success means to you, The Growth Game will be an effective self-coaching tool for a very self-disciplined person. In a self-coaching capacity, it is best to follow the steps of Affirmation, Awareness, Action and Activity Adjustments, Acceleration and Accountability. If you are dedicated to improving yourself and can connect your daily activities to a longer term goal, you will be more apt to look at each day with more direction or purpose. "I am at eight points. If I can meet a few more people or internalize some new knowledge before the day is over, I will hit my commitment of eleven points today." Points are positively reinforcing you to do better and can help to affect change.

The DAD System acts as an accountability mirror. It is a universal measuring stick to help in quantifying what you can do today to assist in the pains of delayed gratification. If you want a change in your results, you must be aware of and tweak your input.

Even if you cannot track your activities daily, your weekly reflection time will show your diagnostics. Some may feel that using the DAD System on a weekly basis allows more focused reflection and planning time. Patterns of the learning you are absorbing and what people you are surrounding yourself with will become clear. You will know what changes you need to make, even if those changes require discomfort or discipline. It brings awareness to and documents the learning and interactions that will control the person you are developing into.

Students

Whether in high school or college, students and their parents can learn about each other's exposure to growth through The DAD System. Young students can start to see the importance of building relationships and constant learning. Parents can assist their children in planning while also sharing their DAD reports with their kids—in familiar terms—to set an example of how even adults need to grow every day.

At the college level, career advisors, professors and even mentoring parents can use the tool as a planning and accountability device for students to start developing their contacts and experiences for their desired career paths. Students could also form study groups and establish professional growth habits while they are still developing their paths on campus.

Business Teams or Employee Development

If you are in a small business or corporate environment, using The DAD System will help the efficiency of your teams or departments. As technology advances, more businesses are moving away from traditional workplace environments. More employees have freedom within a framework. It's not about sitting at a desk for exactly eight hours anymore. People are working from home, working from "phone" and are task-based versus time-based.

The DAD System serves as check-in tool for these teams and their managers. Team meetings discussing their DAD reports will create competition between employees as well as provide clarification on what they are learning and who they are meeting. The system will provide more data on the *means* of their work versus just the results. This can help diagnose working trends and allow for more effective solutions. In a mobile work force environment, the DAD reports will help in the transparency of what workers are doing everyday without micromanagement and it will allow teams to leverage knowledge and contacts. It can help keep team camaraderie or assist in more meaningful conversations for managers to have with the employees in a "results only" environment. It can serve as a culture cohesive.

-Games to Play-

The DAD System's primary purpose is to act as a tool that allows you to quantify, identify and change trends that affect your professional and personal growth. You can make a game by setting out point benchmarks you wish to hit each day, week, or month. You simply win if you achieve your point goals and lose if you don't. This will aid in creating feelings that should promote more exposure to growth. Regardless of the outcome, the tracking- and activity-driven days will help you.

If you want a more literal interpretation of the word game and need to hold yourself accountable, jump into a competition with other people who are serious about their professional or personal development. Start a game with your peers, colleagues or friends. Forming a study group is one of the most impactful things you can do, but let's look at some ways to keep the games fresh. All games abide by an honor system. Remember, the purpose is to help you develop. What's the point in cheating yourself?

Playing Against Others

When playing against another person, you may choose total sum format or match play format. Total sum format will simply add up the points for a time frame and see which individual or team has the most at the end of a designated period. In match play format, you first select an odd number of days to compete. Think of a best of five or seven series in professional sports. At the end of each day, the two competitors would see who had more points. The participant with the higher points for that day is awarded a match point. If you chose a five-day competition then whoever wins three match points would win the match. If you chose a seven-day competition, then the first to four, etc.

Once you have an average number of points per day formulated, you can compare it with a competitor before starting the match. If one competitor has a substantially higher daily point average then you can handicap the match and create a point spread to make it more even. This could be helpful if one participant is in a career or time of their life where they are able to meet more people and have more flexibility than the other person they are competing against.

Combined Match Play

In Combined Team Match Play (2+ players on each team), the competition will come over an odd number of days as stated before. At the end of each day, each team will tally their points. Whichever team had more points gets a match point. The team with the most match points in the allowed period of time wins. Team Match Play prevents one team from running away with the competition due to one monstrous day, (or losing the competition based on one, abnormally awful day.)

"Better Day" Match Play

In "Better Day" Match Play, you simply take the highest score from all the individuals on your team and use that as your representing team score. You would match this against the highest representing score from the other team. Whichever team's score is higher for that day is awarded a match point. The team that has the most match points over a selected odd number of playing days wins.

For example, Aaron and Andy are two participants on Team A and Bob and Bill are the two players on Team B. They selected Better Day Match Play over a 5-day period. At the end of the first day, Aaron has 6 points, while Andy has 8. Andy had the better day, so they would take 8 as their score. On the first day Bob had 7 and Bill had 11 points. Team B would take Bill's points of 11 and compare that to Andy's 8. Team B would have won that day and received a match point. First team to achieve 3 match points in this example would win the contest. Days in which the top two scores from each team are identical, you would use the other teammates score as a tiebreaker.

Blind Categories

Blind Categories adds an element of luck and frustration to the game. The two competing parties would have to designate a non-biased, third party referee. Before the start of the match, the referee would write down which categories would count for each day and then seal his answers in an envelope. The referee would not show this to the competing parties. After the two competing individuals or teams have completed their week, they would open the envelope. Here would show what categories of points counted for each day. Whoever had the most points based on the configured categories would win.

If the competition was over five days, the referee would select one category of points that will count for each day. For example, the referee could choose new experiences to be the measuring tool for Monday, affirmations for Tuesday, knowledge for Wednesday, new connections for Thursday and relationship builders on Friday. Whichever individual had more points in the selected category for the appropriate day would get a match point. This game adds luck and surprise, and requires the competitors to be balanced in every DAD category.

Category Players

In a team competition, Category Players refers to assigning each member of the team to certain DAD categories. If you have five players on each team, each player can take a category (minus meals). If you have fewer than five, you can break it up where some players take on multiple categories. This can be an effective development game when you put players in categories that they are not comfortable for them. It promotes growth in an environment where you don't want to let your team down. At the end of the day or allowed time, you would add all the points together.

For example, if team A had Aaron, Andy and Alex, they would each take two DAD categories for their team. At the end of the time period, a total team score would be based on what the teammates had in their respective assigned categories.

Focused Category

In a team environment, a team leader or manager can set out a certain category with a specific focus. Meaning, if the company is looking to acquire company ABC as a client, then they could make a competition where only points that assist the team in getting closer to that goal, would count. So new connection points would only count if that connection had a tie to ABC. Knowledge points would only count if the information was in regards to company ABC, etc.

-FAQ-

Q: What is the most impactful lesson learned from The Growth Game?

A: You cannot hit what you cannot see. The DAD System brings forward an awareness of daily targets for your exposure to growth. It makes each day more focused and deliberate and aids in alleviating the pain of immediate gratification.

Q: If you have a meal with three different people, how do you score that?

A: Only count the meal once. But if you advanced relationships with different people, score those as separate relationship builder points.

Q: If you reacquaint with an old friend, how is that scored?

A: If you just saw them out at a bar or just accepted them as a friend on Facebook, then treat it as a new connection (only once). If you spent time with this person then treat it as a relationship builder.

Q: If you go on vacation or spend time with the same people over a certain period of time, how do you treat that?

A: Remember, in the personal space, this is a self-coaching tool. So a lot of it is in your hands. However, if you went on a vacation with three close friends and spent time with them, I would only count the meals and relationship builders once.   But I would track new experience points every time the group experienced something new and impactful.   Example: Sky diving, climbing ancient ruins and ordering native food could all be counted as new experience points.

Q: Where does physical exercise fit in?

A: The DAD System was intended for professional and personal growth more than physical growth or habits. Even though the effects of physical fitness can greatly help other areas of your life, fitting it into your DAD System can be tricky.   Training with another person can help in relationship builder points, and meeting people at a gym can help new connection points.   Reading or listening to books on tape while working out can lead to knowledge points.   Breaking your personal best time, repetition, or weight can be a new experience.   Building your vision statement into your MP3 player and listening while on the treadmill can be a clever way to gather some affirmation points as well.

Q: I don't have time to track daily. What can I do?

A: Track weekly. Set aside time, even for 15 minutes on the weekend to reflect on your week. This is probably even more powerful than *rushed* daily tracking.

Q: Can I treat a five-minute phone conversation, a lengthy email, and a 30-minute face-to-face meeting all as relationship builders?

A: Yes, as long as you are advancing the relationship. Again, this is a self-coaching tool so you can be strict or liberal with your definitions. But make sure if you are challenging another person to play the game that you share your definitions.

Q: Can you ever get negative points?

A: No. The system is to act as positive reinforcement to growth.

Q: How do I count reading a book towards my knowledge points?

A: Anytime there is a critical point made that you can internalize, connect to a relevant goal or relationship, and rearticulate in your own words, use that as a knowledge point. Maybe each chapter that you read in a business book brings forward an idea that can help you. If you can reiterate that idea and see how it applies to you, your family, or your team, and be able to paraphrase and put into your own words, then you should count that in your knowledge points. If you just go online and read random facts that you have no use for, then I would be careful how you count those.

Q: If I learn about anything, does that count as a knowledge point?

A: You might want to develop a focus percentage to your DAD points. Meaning, track all knowledge points that you have achieved, but at the end of each week or month, see what percentage of the knowledge you acquired is relevant to your current quest or most passionate goal. For example, if you had 10 knowledge points in a week and only two of the knowledge points were relevant to your most passionate goal or important task at hand, then your focus percentage would only be 20 percent. You may want to look at being more selective with your learning in the upcoming week, unless you had more free time.

Q: How often should a group have multiplier meetings?

A: No correct answer here. Weekly? Monthly? As long as you keep the period of time consistent, and have different topics or contests, they should be effective.

Q: I picture growth in more of a spiritual way with my own definitions. Is the DAD System still applicable?

A: You can still use the system, but all points should be tested or scored based on how you perceive growth. For example, if spirituality is most important to you, you can use the system to track new connections to people who share the same beliefs as you. Or only count relationship builder points when you meet with people that can help you grow spiritually in some way. Same thing with knowledge and new experiences— just make sure the focus is on learning and meeting people that will help you grow the way you perceive growth.

-Notes-

Chapter One

O. Alfred Granum, "Building a Financial Services
Clientele" (Cincinnati,: National Underwriter 10TH edition
1968-2006)

Chapter Three

1. Payscale Human Capital
Brassfield, Margaret. March 2012. "Latest Telecommuting
Statistics Reveal…"
http://www.payscale.com/career-
news/2012/03/working-from-home

2. Bloomberg Business Week
Borenstein, Nathaniel. January 2012. "Forget the Office"
http://www.businessweek.com/debateroom/archives/201
2/01/forget_the_office_let_employees_work_from_home
.html

3. Chicago Tribune (from web)
   Samuelson, Kristin. February 2012. "Retaining Gen Y Employees"
http://articles.chicagotribune.com/2012-02-05/business/ct-biz-0205-outside-opinion-gen-y-20120205_1_baby-boomers-workplace-generation-x-employees

Chapter Six

Optify Software Whitepaper, "The Change Face of SERPS" 2012

-About the Author-

Eddy Ricci is the director of a unique training and development collaborative platform that services four financial planning firms in New England where he has arguably worked with more new, Gen Y financial professionals than anyone in the country over the past three years. He is also the founder of the DAD System and The Growth Game, LLC., a professional development company.

Eddy is a certified coach and specializes in helping professionals develop sales skills and implement business development activity systems. He has also served on national field training committees and has had articles published in industry leadership journals. Eddy also holds his FINRA Series 7, 66, 9, and 10 licenses as well for investment and NYSE branch office supervision. In the past, Eddy has worked with HBO, various publications and founded Big Hope Films, a non-profit film project for disabled young adults. Big Hope Film's project was screened at the 2009 Rhode Island International Film Festival. He is a graduate of New York University and is a member of the NYU Young Alumni Leadership Circle. Eddy is married and currently resides in Rhode Island.

er@thegrowthgame.com

For Access to DAD System software, group sales or Quick Guides for your teams, students or study groups and additional exercises please visit our website

www.thegrowthgame.com

"Life is 10% what happens to you and 90% how you react." – Charles Swindoll

"There are no traffic jams on the extra mile." – Zig Ziglar

"If you could kick the person in the pants responsible for most of your trouble, you wouldn't be able to sit for a month."- Theodore Roosevelt

Reader Notes:

_____

_____

_____

_____

_____

_____

_____

_____

_____

_____

_____

_____

_____

_____